Construction Audit

Construction Audit is becoming more and more prevalent, and organizations are appreciating its importance. Learning the basics of construction auditing can provide valuable knowledge and skills for professionals and students in the construction industry, offering insights into financial management, risk mitigation, compliance and overall project oversight.

This book is not just for auditors, however. It could be used by project managers, integrity monitors, construction managers and anyone else who wants to understand the elements that go into creating a successful project. Legal teams involved in contracting and overpayment recovery will also benefit.

This book:

- Walks you through all phases of construction; starting with project inception. It will guide the reader through all the processes and the risks in each of these.
- Will guide the reader through the many challenges they will face throughout life of the project. This book provides real-life solutions to common problems in construction.
- Introduces project management techniques, while not concentrating on a special methodology, the book builds on project management fundamentals. Understanding this will help enable the reader to talk to project managers more effectively.
- Defines the components of a successful project and gives the reader the tools needed to ensure these components.
- Uses real-life examples of control breakdowns, errors or fraud.
- Will help readers build an audit strategy and plan by understanding risks and effective controls that can be implemented to mitigate risk.

Whether tackling your first project or your 21st project, this book will help you think outside the box and understand the finite processes and pieces of your project. There is always room for something new, new perspectives or improvement, and this book will help you find it.

Security, Audit and Leadership Series

Series Editor: Dan Swanson, Dan Swanson and Associates, Ltd., Winnipeg, Manitoba, Canada.

The ***Security, Audit and Leadership Series*** publishes leading-edge books on critical subjects facing security and audit executives as well as business leaders. Key topics addressed include Leadership, Cybersecurity, Security Leadership, Privacy, Strategic Risk Management, Auditing IT, Audit Management and Leadership

Modern Management and Leadership: Best Practice Essentials with CISO/CSO Applications
Mark Tarallo

Rising from the Mailroom to the Boardroom: Unique Insights for Governance, Risk, Compliance and Audit Leaders
Bruce Turner

Operational Auditing: Principles and Techniques for a Changing World (Second Edition)
Hernan Murdock

CyRM℠: Mastering the Management of Cybersecurity
David X Martin

Why CISOs Fail (Second Edition)
Barak Engel

Riding the Wave: Applying Project Management Science in the Field of Emergency Management
Andrew Boyarsky

The Shortest Hour: An Applied Approach to Boardroom Governance of Cybersecurity
Lee Parrish

Global Audit Leadership: A Practical Approach to Leading a Global Internal Audit (GIA) Function in a Constantly Changing Internal and External Landscape
Audley L. Bell

Construction Audit: Building a Solid Foundation
Denise Cicchella

For more information about this series, please visit: https://www.routledge.com/Internal-Audit-and-IT-Audit/book-series/CRCINTAUDITA

Construction Audit
Building a Solid Foundation

Denise Cicchella

CRC Press
Taylor & Francis Group
Boca Raton London New York

CRC Press is an imprint of the
Taylor & Francis Group, an **informa** business

Designed cover image: © Shutterstock

First edition published 2025
by CRC Press
2385 NW Executive Center Drive, Suite 320, Boca Raton FL 33431

and by CRC Press
4 Park Square, Milton Park, Abingdon, Oxon, OX14 4RN

CRC Press is an imprint of Taylor & Francis Group, LLC

ISBN: 978-1-032-61003-0 (hbk)
ISBN: 978-1-032-61004-7 (pbk)
ISBN: 978-1-003-46148-7 (ebk)

DOI: 10.1201/9781003461487

Typeset in Sabon
by SPi Technologies India Pvt Ltd (Straive)

Disclaimer

Case studies in this writing are actual cases and findings experienced by Denise, her students and her colleagues, however facts and names may have been altered. No identification with actual persons or organizations is intended or should be inferred.

Contents

About the author

Denise Cicchella is an experienced consultant and auditor. She is a passionate educator and spreads her knowledge about audit, fraud, project management and other topics via conferences, live presentations and webinars. Denise worked in numerous industries before specializing in construction audit and consultancy. She has worked on numerous construction projects including commercial, residential, healthcare and energy. She has helped her clients recover as much as 10% via construction audits performed. Denise is a Certified Internal Auditor, Certified Fraud Examiner, and Certified Construction Auditor. She is a life member of the National Association of Construction Auditors and is the Founding President of the NY/NJ Chapter. Denise earned her Bachelor's Degree in Accounting from Loyola University in Baltimore, MD, and her Master's in International Business from Fairleigh Dickinson University.

Introduction

Construction audit basics

Construction projects are among the largest and most complex endeavors an organization can undertake. They can have a long-term impact on the organization and efficiencies, or mismanagement can be felt for years to come. If you want to reduce costs, mitigate risk, and gain control of your projects – Construction Audit is the way to do it!

Construction Audit is the process of systematically and independently assessing a construction project to ensure that the owner's best interest is protected. Those who don't recognize its importance will say that it is a justification for the costs of a project. In 1997, Evandro Braz defined Construction Audit for the Project Management Institute (PMI) as a systemic field test to ensure that invoices of direct and indirect costs are proper and correct and are in line with the contracts.[1] Really this is just the tip of the iceberg! Construction projects are often critical to an organization's success. Projects are often material by total expenditure, reputation and an enabler of new services and products. Albeit this study by Braz, was done in the late 1990s, the industry has changed since and Construction Audit is becoming more collaborative.

A good Construction Audit will adopt a holistic approach to ensuring the objectives of the organization are met and the executive committees are getting the information they need about projects. Construction Audit should look at site procedures and policies, audit of wages, review of change orders, review of safety issues, contracting and an investigation into project procurement. In fact, as we will discuss later in this book, there are approximately 45 processes that audit should/could consider. Construction projects are at very high risk. Often, there is waste with money being left on the table, which could be recovered. Strategic imperatives may be lost or forfeited. Reputational damage may occur. Negative events could potentially have been avoided and lessons to be learned for future projects may be lost if Construction Audits are not performed.

A Construction Audit can be for a new site or a capital improvement on an already existing site. Each project is unique; therefore, each audit is as well. I will give you the background necessary to design an audit program

DOI: 10.1201/9781003461487-1

that will work with your project. The fundamentals of my Construction Audit approach rely on effective project management principles and accounting practices.

PMI defines a project as 'temporary efforts to create value through unique products, services and processes.'[2] In essence a project:

- Creates a unique product.
- Has a start date or starting point.
- Has criteria to determine success.
- Has an end date or end event (this is more critical than a start date).
- Projects are normally completed across the organization rather than a single department.
- Projects often involve an element of unfamiliarity.
- A project is in progress toward obtaining a goal; it has a purpose.

A project is a project even if something happens to end it prematurely. A project can be canceled because the project is being mismanaged, there are cost overruns, situations change or just because the organization does not wish to continue. With that in mind, procedures around project management should involve monitoring and reporting of the project as it proceeds from month to month or phase to phase.

In some cases, you may want to use audits as part of gatekeeping procedures – as each milestone is reached, or periodically, a temperature check is done to consider if the project should proceed and is meeting expectations. Historically there are examples of projects that were badly managed, or cost overruns were extreme; these are projects that could have benefitted from periodic reviews. We will talk about some of those projects.

In some organizations, project audit may be an integral part of the organization's normal operations. Lessons learned and cost minimization will be critical objectives of audits. In these cases, a Construction Audit should still be done but you will have the added advantage that there are, hopefully, procedures in place as to how project procedures are done, and then the audit becomes an exercise in compliance. Though I encourage audit to examine the procedures being applied and to apply operational audit procedures as well. Clearing unneeded red tape can be beneficial. Ideally these procedures, at a minimum, should contain procedures around many of the different processes that we will see in Chapter 4.

A project should be assigned a project executive or executive sponsor. This person will be pivotal in ensuring that someone is providing executive oversight and facilitates project progress when roadblocks are encountered. The sponsor will be a sounding board to and from the executive committee.

A project should also be backed by what is known as a project charter. The charter should specify established requirements for the project, the general makeup of the team, skills that will be outsourced and any goals the project is expected to meet. It should establish deadlines. This charter is usually found within the project file and may be referred to or even attached to the contract with the general contractor. In some cases, a redacted copy is attached.

Let's start by dispelling some myths.

Myth #1 – I have often heard it said that *a Construction Audit is not needed if there is a construction manager or outsourced project manager*. In either case, a construction manager is usually paid their fee as a percentage of monthly costs. The more cost generated, the greater their fee. There is no incentive for them to find savings or cost overruns; there is no independence. Auditors are independent of the project. They have made none of the decisions on the project, nor do they have a financial incentive in the project.

In fact, they can take it to the next step – they can/should audit the costs of the construction manager, as well. Lastly, remember what I said about Braz's definition. It is not just about the financials.

Myth #2 – *I have a lump sum contract so there is no need to do an audit.* While you reduce one risk, financial risk, there are so many other aspects of the project that can and should still be audited. And note, yes, I did say lump sum will REDUCE your risk. It will not eliminate it; it may even be the wrong choice in respect to other aspects of your project. And again, it is not just about the financials.

Myth #3 – *There is no need to do an audit, as this is just a one-off thing.* Many lessons can be learned when doing a Construction Audit that will aid your organization in project management, procurement and maybe even accounting for other projects – even if they are non-construction. Additionally, the amount you spend on construction is often a material amount, and it should be audited. Even if the project is a one-off now, there may be similar projects in the pike where you can apply some of the lessons learned during this first review. In fact, an audit can show control weaknesses in the overall project management procedures.

Myth #4 – *Auditing my project will hurt my relationship with my construction team.* In truth, increasing transparency will show the team you are interested in what they are doing. If a team member has faith in their work, they will not fear an audit and will be more collaborative, will be more communicative and will foster a culture of truth and honesty. In some cases, audit can clear some roadblocks that the team is experiencing.

Myth #5 – *Auditing the project will create a slow down at the project and besides, auditors can get hurt.* The fact that an auditor can get hurt auditing a construction site may be true, but when we talk about safety, I will show you how to minimize that risk. Besides most of the audit can be done off-site. As for slowing down progress, sometimes an audit can help progress, they can help settle disputes, move barriers along and can help defend certain points with management. Audit should still be mindful of the inconvenience their participation may be and work to keeping out of the way. Not every auditor, especially those who are untrained or who have never been on a site, needs to go on-site unless they are doing a site walkthrough.

This book will dispel these myths and more. It will guide you through the phases of a project, the phases of an audit, contract analysis, sample audit steps, examples of fraud and applying earned value management tools. We will also cover risk and those most prevalent for each phase discussed.

NOTES

1 Braz, E.F. (1997) Construction audits: Scorekeeping that wins. *PM Network*, *11*(11), 31–33.
2 What is Project Management|PMI.

Chapter 1

Types of construction

Knowing the type of construction you are auditing is important. It enables you to have a conceptual understanding of the potential risks that may arise. It can act as a starting point for researching specific risks that you may encounter. It will also facilitate an easier flow of communication with the rest of the construction team. Knowing the type of construction may be needed when researching or understanding building code compliance.

Construction is not a one-size-fits-all scenario; there are almost infinite possibilities. Each project is unique and architects (possibly with the support of engineers or other specialists) design the building based on where the building will be located and its primary use. There are several basic types of construction that you may encounter:

1. *Building construction* – Building construction has the goal of creating a building that will serve a future purpose. This can vary from dormitories, hospitals, business buildings, apartment buildings, malls, etc. It can be further broken into residential, commercial and institutional.

   Residential construction would be a house, dormitory, apartment or anything where the goal is to live and cook in the facility.

   Commercial construction may include residential elements, but the goal of the constructed entity is to make income or provide a service – rent, profit sharing, straight income, etc. Examples include nursing homes and senior care facilities.

   Institutional is very similar to residential but considers buildings where people may live but other services are also offered. Prisons and schools are examples of institutional construction.
2. *Engineering construction* – Engineering construction is the building of a facility or area that will be used to supply a service such as airports, hospitals, roads, reservoirs and highways, to name a few categories. Projects carry significant reputational risk as they are public, often funded with taxpayer money and any significant issues are likely to attract adverse media comments. It is a highly complex type of construction with numerous working parts. It would normally be

DOI: 10.1201/9781003461487-2

completed using a cost-plus contract due to all the small details that only emerge as construction proceeds. (See chapter on Contracts.)

One example of an engineering construction was the Central Artery Tunnel Project in Boston. It was subject to large overpayments (originally budgeted for $2.5 billion, it wound up costing $14.8 billion.) and completed almost nine years later than planned. It became infamous and the project was nicknamed the 'Big Dig.' This highlighted and emphasized the risk of reputational harm from public projects.

A lot of engineering construction is harmed by a 'Not in my Neighborhood Mentality.' The service is needed in the area, but the neighbors don't want it there. Hospitals are sometimes faced with this issue. Power plants are another.

3. *Industrial construction* – Industrial construction is the type of construction that builds things such as factories and manufacturing plants. Shipbuilding is another example of industrial construction. Due to the size and complexity of these projects, they most often are also heavy construction projects.
4. *Expansionary* – Expansionary projects are generally not as expensive as other types of construction as you have an existing facility (with all its underlying infrastructure) and the project can be anything from a new wing, a new room, the conversion of a shell room or even what we term an in-fill building. An in-fill takes an existing building and 'fills in' any unused space with a new area. So, if you had an L-shaped building, an infill would make it a rectangle. It could come with either new infrastructure or would connect to the existing infrastructure. Usually connecting the infrastructure is the last step in the project, meaning (ideally) there is little disruption to existing tenants (or other users) while construction is ongoing.
5. *Repair* – Repair projects take an existing structure and modernize, repair, extend its life, or, otherwise upgrade it. Usually repair projects are major repairs that take months or years and may require temporary ceases of operations.
6. *Heavy construction* – Heavy construction is not a construction type, but rather a description used of any of the above types of construction where the construction itself is very specialized and requires the extra attention of civil engineers and specialty equipment. Heavy construction examples include ports, roads, bridges, dams, water-handling facilities and energy-producing facilities.
7. *Hybrid projects* – Hybrid projects are a combination of the types that we mention here. With airport construction, if you are constructing a new terminal, it would be hybrid as the runway would be engineering and the kiosks inside the terminal would be building construction. Burj Khalifa is an example of a hybrid project as it combines office space, hotel space (Armani Hotel), residences, lounges, pools and restaurants.

8. *Miscellaneous or undefined* – There are some custom projects that fall into none of the above categories. This is due to the level of customization. The type of construction may be defined in the contracts or can be clarified by the architect. Knowing the type of construction is needed as building codes or other regulations may apply to only certain types of buildings.

CONSTRUCTION WAYS AND MEANS: THE METHOD OF CONSTRUCTION

Ways and means refers to how the construction will actually occur, what material will be used and all the details of the construction. The auditor is not to opine on the ways and means, they are not qualified too. The ways and means are the responsibility of the architect, engineer or architect-engineer. These experts will normally determine the type of construction that will be used. The type of construction will change based on where the project is going to be and considers a lot of the geological risks associated with that location – fires, tornadoes, hurricanes, normal weather patterns, etc. The end use of the project is also a consideration. Common methods include:

- *Steel framed* – If you are building in an area where weather is extreme and random, steel-framed construction may be exactly what you need. It is common for office buildings to be steel framed. In humid or marine environments, steel deterioration can occur so additional thoughts on coating or reinforcing the steel should be considered.

  It is cheaper and faster to fire protect the steel frame in situ, but it causes too many breaks in the coating, compromising durability in the long run. Some local building codes may specify if in situ coating is allowed. Steel, however, presents another risk. In times of geopolitical instability, the price or availability of steel fluctuates. Most steel is sourced from overseas. Currently, a lot of steel comes from Russia and because of ongoing political conflicts in the area, steel supply is slow. Many projects are delayed due to this.
- *ICF* (insulated concrete framework) *or PIF* (permanently insulated framework) – ICF originated in Germany and is similar to a 'Lego' system. Giant blocks are pieced together and then filled with foam insulation. It is very versatile as the foam can even be installed in cold environments. Its ability to keep out the cold and preserve heat makes it ideal for new warehouse builds and many other project types. ICF when cured is more durable than steel constructed buildings. This is an ideal construction technique for irregularly shaped buildings.
- *Brick and block* – Brick and block uses internal blockwork such as cinder block and external brick or stone. This is often the cheapest method but not necessarily the sturdiest.

- *Timber frame* – This is a common method and often when seeing new construction in the United States you will see this. The frame of the building is put up, and it is then covered in a breathable membrane. Insulation is placed between the beams via sheeting or now, more commonly, foam.
- *Closed* – In a closed frame construction, it is a combination of panels, studs and rails. Insulation such as lined sheeting is used. It is then covered with a vapor barrier on the 'warm' side of the house and a breathing membrane is put on the outer face of the building. This configuration makes the building more energy efficient but is not recommended for areas where excess moisture is possible.
- *Cob construction* – Cob construction is rising in popularity, as it is seen as the most environmentally friendly of the other construction types. In cob construction, a sludge of soil, water, silt, clay, straw, flint or sand (aka – DIRT!) is used to shape walls and dry. Walls will be built up over time with layers of this sludge, allowing them to dry and then 'plastering' them with clay or lime. Some are even using hemp as a binder. You may even find it unfinished.

  It is simple and cheap but results in a very hard and resilient finish, which is energy efficient in terms of insulation. It is, however, very time-consuming, and construction in bad weather may need to be suspended. Imagine it like a gigantic sandcastle but the tide is coming in. Examples of COB buildings can be seen in Arizona and New Mexico – the adobe structures built by Native Americans are generally COB buildings or in the UK residential market. You may find buildings that use partial COB construction, especially where high fire usage is seen; i.e. heavy manufacturing plants. You will find them all over the world.
- *Straw bale* – Straw bale construction is when builders create a generic skeleton – not too much needed – just a general outline. This outline is generally wood or steel. Bales of straw, hay or other materials are stacked high and wide, reinforced with steel posts and wiring, and used to create structural frames or as insulation between beams. It results in a fire-resistant building that is waterproof and pest free. The problem is if moisture gets into the walls, it can lead to toxic mildew formation inside the building, and if this happens, the remedy is time-consuming and expensive.

Learning these various ways and means will enable the auditor to visualize what the construction team is saying when they discuss designs used and pricing. Additionally, it can become a significant element when auditing an owner's presentations to prospective lenders, investors and capital markets. To preserve funding and remain in compliance, auditors want to ensure presentations made were accurate, including the type of construction used. When we talk about risks, certain types present different risks and knowing the type of construction will aid in the risk exercise.

Chapter 2

General risks

Before you start the audit and plan it, you need to assess the risks involved with the project. Your project manager should have already completed an assessment. I always like to do my own to ensure that the risk assessment of the project manager is thorough, as it often is not. I have seen risk assessments that only list six or seven risks. A construction project has a lot more than a handful of risks. Audit may enjoy a more strategic perspective of risk. In practice, the Project Manager may miss risks, particularly if the pm is new or an external consultant. The other reason I like to compare them is the project manager has likely prioritized the risk; again, I like to validate this to make sure it aligns with the organization's strategic objectives for the project. Audit is well placed to identify the wider impacts of risks.

There are different approaches to risk identification. From a project manager perspective, these are often recorded in a risk register. In audit terms, this may be a risk matrix. They are comparable documents that serve the same purpose.

The auditor should use the project risk register as a starting point. While many risks may be similar from project to project the auditor should be wary of using generic risk assessments. Each project is unique and as a result each project has different risks and different risk priorities. There are general project risks that exist for all projects. To determine these risks, ask yourself, 'What will make the executives happy and deem the project a success?' We discuss this in the *Pillars of Success* chapter (Chapter 5). As you will see, when we discuss project appraisal, you will learn that the answer to this question can be found on the project approval paperwork (or it should, if procedures are followed and require that level of transparency) or in the project charter. If it is not documented, talk to the executive sponsor and find out what the consensus of the executives is.

To confuse it even more, the risks will change based on the phase of construction that the project is in. Timing risks may likely be strong at the beginning, but as deadlines are hit early, the priority of the timing risk lessens – as remember risks are two pronged: impact and probability. Timing risk can be enumerated as you will see in the *Earned Value Management* chapter (Chapter 17).

DOI: 10.1201/9781003461487-3

There are other types of risk that get folded into the project but the above are the pillars of the overall project. Other risks include:

REPUTATIONAL

Pick up a newspaper or listen to a news show and you will see a construction failure or a site that is on the radar screen for falling behind. Protecting your reputation must be on the mindset of the executives and the more successful the project, the more you will be able to reach that goal. There is also the possibility of being 'guilty by association.'

I was working with a client who received negative press on their project as the contractor was sued for sexual harassment. This occurred prior to my client having a business relationship with the contractor but when the indictment was handed down, the contractor was on-site for my client. Protestors who had followed the case picketed the client's site when they saw the contractor's van. The client did not know about the indictment, and it is possible they could have won the bid even if they did know about the indictment. The only action my client could have taken was to terminate the vendor right away. The vendor had been deeply entrenched in the project and it would not be possible to replace them quickly. The client was left in a position where they had to juggle which risk (reputational vs financial) was the priority to maintain.

Even with risks being identified early on, it is critical that risk management continues to be forefront of all project communications. New risks may be emerging and the quicker they are addressed, the less the damage (hopefully). It should be addressed in monthly project reports, it should be discussed at weekly construction meetings, it should be mentioned at daily foreman meetings, and any new or emerging risks should be noted on the daily reports, and subsequently month-end reporting. The earlier an emerging risk is identified, the easier it is to mitigate this risk. These communication methods will be expanded on later.

FINANCIAL

When they hear construction audit, many will automatically think of the risk over finances. I have had seasoned veterans tell me that they know they will go over budget – it's 'just the cost of doing business.' In a way, these veterans are not wrong. In the United Kingdom, fewer than one in three projects come in within 10% of their initial budgeted amount and 69% of all construction projects go over budget.[1] Most projects go over budget because of the following:

- Inadequate project design – Project design and project budgets are based on estimates and many times these are off. It is hard to pinpoint exactly how many hours a project will take; small inaccuracies can cause large deviations in finance. When deciding between costs, contractors tend to side on the side of optimism, leaving owners at a loss. Project designs are based on what is known. The unknowns can throw off both design and cost.

- Scope creep – Scope creep is related to inadequate project design and often involves a change of opinion or a contractor who can convince an owner that they need a few unplanned extras. Examples of scope creep would be a contractor telling an owner that instead of having pine doors they need oak for durability instead.
- Inadequate management of construction site – Construction sites can be subject to many interfering forces – weather, tenants, traffic, etc. and not all of these forces can be controlled. These can cause delays and the need for overtime which will increase cost.
- Lack of oversight – There is a lot going on during construction projects and a person can spend all day in meetings about the project. This means they can't be at the site overseeing everything. Then once a month they get a bill that needs to be checked, approved, and paid in a short amount of time. Errors happen and may go undetected. Having a construction controller or an audit going on during the construction will provide some of that oversight and hopefully gain control.
- Issues with vendors – Part of construction management can be attributed to playing referee among vendors. Relationships can sometimes turn into power struggles or each vendor thinks they take priority over any other vendor. Well-defined roles and responsibilities can help overcome some of these issues.
- Delay in permitting and inspection – Delays happen all the time and it is up to the project manager to work around them. Some just can't be fixed and it requires that workers just hang around until the delay fixes itself. In the Central Artery Tunnel Projects, workers waited over a week as management on the project forgot to secure clearance for them to enter part of the site.

There are other reasons why projects go over, and these are just a few examples.

FRAUD

A project can sometimes cultivate conditions for fraud. This is because the project is high profile and fast-moving, and it includes many small details. The Association of Certified Fraud Examiners states that for fraud to happen you need three things – motive, opportunity and rationalization.

- Motive exists as contractors claim they low bid to get the work, so they are entitled to some extras. They need to make up for what they had to bid to get the job.

- The opportunity exists because no two projects are ever 100% alike and this means it is hard to compare costs, performance and budgets, allowing fraud to hide, sometimes in plain sight. There is also a lot of pressure on these projects so sometimes owners allow the fraud just so the project will get done or they do not have the time and resources to scrutinize every detail. If an organization is doing a project and they normally never do construction it may be hard for them to find any concealments nor do they have the confidence to question.
- Rationalization exists as each contractor realizes what a huge bucket of money is being spent on the project – no one will notice a little extra skimming. Would they?

Common frauds seen are:

- Embezzlement and fictitious vendors
- Payroll schemes, including ghost employees
- Vendor or Subcontractor kickbacks
- Theft of job-site materials
- Corruption (bribery, extortion and bid-rigging)
- Change order falsifications.

I talk about many of the frauds that can occur throughout this book. One example of an area where fraud is prevalent:

An invoice comes in for labor. The rates are not what is agreed in the contract. Most employees are overcharged and some undercharged. The vendor claims in a rush to get started, rates had not been correctly inputted; however, they will do a 'true-up' reconciliation at the end. During the reconciliation they net out the undercharges from the overcharges and all parties think this is the end. However, a year or two later, accounts payable get an invoice for the undercharges found during a 'recent audit,' evidence of the undercharge is attached. The invoice will go to accounts payable rather than the project team. The undercharges get paid for, again. To avoid this, the organization should insist that the rates are corrected at the beginning. Doing a reconciliation at the end is problematic:

- It is hard to prove the true-up reconciliation is correct (accuracy can be affected by employees leaving or getting promoted).
- Who will perform the reconciliation; and are they independent of the project? If performed by the vendor the reconciliation will lack impartiality.
- It is better from an accounting standpoint to correct the rates at the earliest opportunity to ensure that correct cost is allocated at the correct time period.
- If there is an overcharge, the owner of the project is essentially lending money to the contractor, free of charge.

- The accuracy of monthly reporting is important to the project. If labor charges are wrong, monthly reports will contain inaccurate data.
- In the lack of any tickler system, it relies on everyone's memory to do an end-of-project reconciliation. The end of the project may be years away and there is a high likelihood that many members of the team will not be there as the project winds up. This can be more problematic if the person who suggested the reconciliation is gone then you may be stuck. If an employee has been overcharged and leaves the project, will the reconciliation still take them into consideration?

It is hard to get a true statistic on the amount of money wasted on fraud, as there is a fine line between error and fraud. Many owners consider overpayments as errors as long as they recover the amount identified. However, it is so prevalent that the Manhattan district attorney was able to indict 24 individuals and 26 organizations after an eight-year kickback scheme for theft of more than $5 million.[2]

THIRD-PARTY RISK

Third-party risk is the risk that a vendor or participant in the construction is in a situation where they face bankruptcy during the course of your project. Third-party risk becomes more prevalent during times of financial uncertainty. We are faced with a constantly changing business environment and keeping on top of it can mean the difference between the life and death of a vendor. Construction projects can last for years, and though consulting our crystal ball to ensure the vendor will be there to the end would be nice, we have to be prepared that they will not survive. The best control for this risk is proper due diligence before hiring the vendor. So, what things might you want answers to:

- How long have they been in business?
- How financially sound are they?
- Do they have any pending litigation against them?
- Are they licensed (if necessary: many trades in construction require a license)?
- Where do they get their supply from (if they are supplying parts or materials for the project)?
- Do they have staff on hand to handle a project of your size?
- What contingency plans do they have to ensure business continuity? Part of business continuity can be backup plans should the trades go out on strike.
- Can they deliver on project expectations and what they promise when being chosen for the work?

SUPPLY CHAIN RISK

Supply chain risk during construction projects is the risk that the materials or equipment needed for the project cannot be obtained when needed. Construction activity is quick and relies on hitting milestones in their schedule. A task can sometimes be delayed but it may cause a major delay in the whole of the project. Having goods available when you need them is imperative. In an environment of geopolitical uncertainty, construction is going to feel the effects. This is mostly due to the availability of steel. Steel is needed on almost every construction project, and it is usually sourced from overseas. China, India, and Japan are common places to source steel.

The other things you want answered are in relationship to their importance on the project.

- How critical are they to the project?
- What delays can you tolerate?
- What are project expectations?
  - Would the project fail if the third party fails?
- How hard would it be to get a replacement vendor?
  - How soon can the replacement be brought up to speed on the project?
- How flexible is the schedule if goods are not available?
- Are there alternatives available?

If a third party is deemed critical to the success of the project, then the increased need for due diligence comes into play. It may also require that you get creative to compensate or ensure third-party success. Some of the solutions I have seen:

- Three project managers were hired for a project (a project manager is one of the hardest to replace quickly). All three were from different companies. If one company failed, the project leaders were confident that the other two companies could continue to manage the project without continuity issues. There were conditions in place that stated if one contractor failed, they would be replaced, and the other two contractors would be responsible for bringing the third company up to date. Though this situation would help if one party went insolvent, it did increase overall cost.
- A project was being done in an area where there was a lot of economic uncertainty. The project had to be done and it could not wait for better economic times. The construction manager was hired with the contingency that in case of financial failure, the project owner would support any costs necessary for that project and ensure the company would not

fail. They would be bailed out but only for this particular project. Should a bail out occur, money to keep the company afloat would be put into a restrictive bank account in the name of the contractor and the owner. All checks would require signature of the owner and the contractor.

- A company was believed to be 'borrowing' money from the project to pay expenses of another project. They were considered a key vendor to be terminated so they opened a bank account where payments to the company would go and any expenses on the project were to be used from this account. Signatures of the project owner and construction company were required on all outgoing checks.
- Two organizations were joint owners of a property. They were working on one project, and each hired their own Project Manager; this way they could have their own independent eyes on the project. This helped keep the Project Managers honest, as well. They worked together as one, but each represented one-half of the owners.
- When the Burj Khalifa project was underway in Dubai, significant construction was done throughout the city. To ensure availability of concrete, a dedicated concrete facility plant was built on-site.[3]

If continuity is a concern, you can require that the vendor take out a surety bond. A surety bond is an insurance policy, of sorts, where the surety company will reimburse you if the third party fails or fails to meet the requirements of the project. The issue with surety bonds in recent times is ensuring that the surety holder survives. They used to have to be a rated company but after the financial crisis, reliance on these ratings has fallen.

REGULATORY RISK

There are various rules and regulations around construction sites, and it can be difficult to keep on top of all these codes, especially if this is the first construction an owner is doing. They go down to building codes, Federal aviation regulations, union rules and guidance, liability for injury, and possibly even requirements by industry regulators.

The Federal Aviation Administration (FAA) requires a permit on construction cranes any time that they will exceed a 100:1 sloped surface from the nearest point of the nearest runway out to 20,000 feet or 200 feet AGL (above ground level) beyond. Regulatory forms must be submitted to the FAA at least 30 days before or more either before the date the proposed construction is to begin, or the date an application for a construction permit is to be filed. Failure to file on time can cause the start of the construction to be delayed. Additionally, you must notify them if the construction will be greater than 200 feet above sea level.[4]

I have had several clients who did not know about the FAA requirements and did not file with the FAA. There are additional requirements if operating near known flight life paths. The requirements as I just spelled them out are technical, and the project owner may not have the expertise to realize what they needed to file and what to file. For this reason, it is preferable to make the filing of permits and variances the responsibility of the project manager or the architect. They likely have more expertise in this arena. However, the owner should at least question whether all paperwork has been filed, as well they should have duplicate copies for their files.

Due to the complexity and height of Burj Khalifa in Dubai, FAA reporting had to be done as the progress of the building had different impacts on flight patterns.

PERIMETER ACCESS

Access to the site should be protected for several reasons. Firstly, there are a lot of equipment and material on the site that you would want to protect from being stolen. Some of this material and equipment can be dangerous if used incorrectly. This is especially important if you have any gases or flammable material. In the wrong hands, this can be dangerous to property, the project and people.

Copper is a magnet for theft on a project – very valuable and very often found on construction sites. There are people who will walk active and inactive sites to find copper to steal. They will even go so far as to strip it out of insulated wire. They leave the insulation behind but take the copper. Copper is a very versatile material and is used in many trades, making it very easy to resell. It exists in electrical wires, fuses, plumbing, phone lines, IT cables, etc. at the cost of about $3.6 per unit,[5] and the resale value of copper is enticing. Scrap yards should ask for identification but are often laxed to do so. Copper is sent to places like China and India and then used in the manufacturing of other products.

Besides the value of the copper is the risk it puts on the site as to the safety of thieves. They often do not wear the correct protective gear and may use a saw that creates a spark or kickback injuring the thief. Some are stealing without actual removal of the outer wire, resulting in just the insulation with no conduit. This would, of course, open vulnerability to the quality of the end project and will need to be searched for and replaced – all of which can eat up valuable time (and cost). It cannot be relied on that workers would notice the missing cooper, as they may not be looking for it.

The top five items stolen from construction sites are copper, lumber, small tools, heavy machinery and aluminum.[6] Lumber and aluminum generally do not have tracking numbers on them and even if they did, the theft of either of these items would likely stay below the radar as they are common items and easy to conceal or explain. Aluminum can be sold as scrap metal.

Small tools can be stolen and then resold on open sites as used equipment. Open sites would be Amazon or Facebook Marketplace. Heavy machinery, unlike the rest, is a bit harder to conceal both during the theft and after the theft. Most people would probably look twice if a stolen bulldozer was coming down the road. But even so, with companies renting out heavy equipment, it can still go unnoticed. Think about what happens if someone is redoing a driveway or home construction. You see equipment but just write it off as something to do the work. Few of us would go – '"Wow, that might be stolen goods.' Or 'Hey, the owner works construction, I am sure he stole that from one of his sites.'

How would you mitigate this risk? There are certain controls that can be used. For heavy machinery and copper spools, organizations have begun to

- Add GPS trackers
- Lock chains through the wheels or spools
- Keep them in a circle to make it harder to steal and easier to spot anything missing
- Barriers are placed near the equipment
- Park Equipment near the center of the site rather than on the perimeter.

For all-over perimeter access, the first control is fencing. Fencing should be all around the property and should include a solid tarpaulin so that no one or nothing can use the links to try and get past it. Holes in the tarpaulin should be looked for and promptly fixed every day. An essential task on the site should be for someone to walk the perimeter daily and check for said holes or missing links. It would be easy (and unsafe) for a young child to access a site if links are missing or there are holes at the bottom. However, I have seen sites where they check the perimeter at eye level and miss gaps on the bottom or they walk the perimeter but are distracted and not paying attention. Let's face it, it may not be the most exciting task, but it is a very important task. I recommend that the person who checks the perimeter should have to sign a checklist afterward – one for documentation and two for a reminder of its importance. Open issues should be photographed and repaired. Other controls to protect the perimeter include cameras on-site.

Cameras should be controlled to ensure that tapes or media that they record are kept safe. Recordings made should offer a valid view and the picture taken should be well-focused. I worked on a site where the recording quality was great and at the beginning of the project, the view was optimal. Alas, as the project went on and the walls were erected the camera position was never moved. The camera was pointed beautifully at a brick wall! If cameras are used, they should be checked daily or at least weekly to ensure adjustments, if needed, are made. They can be properly positioned but the lens gets dirty or the view is obstructed. We will explore this topic in more detail later.

ESG RISK (CONSTRUCTION MEANS AND METHODS COULD AFFECT CARBON FOOTPRINT)

In an effort to help save the planet from destruction, ESG has been a business decision factor. ESG stands for Environment, Social and Governance. The crux of the issue is what are owners and vendors doing to remain responsible for the environment, social conditions and transparency of administrative tasks. From a construction standpoint, this can reach out to ways and means of construction. When we spoke about construction types, some of the methods are more environmentally friendly. Alternate materials can be used to help meet ESG initiatives. For example, concrete accounts for the erosion of soil and pollution of water due to runoff during storms. Owners may want to think of what alternatives (hemp is more environmentally friendly and can be mixed with lime to mimic concrete) are out there to reduce the amount of concrete on their project. This task should be given to the architect/engineer, before the design phase, if possible.

In project management we have a concept called value engineering. This is where the designers and planners of the project (in our case, architects) take a project down to minute details and try to find hidden savings. With ESG the organization can do the same, but instead of looking for cost savings, they can look for environmental friendliness.

With all these risks, oversight is important. Auditing can be a good oversight tool to use, but only if the audit is being done concurrently with the project (Figure 2.1).

Construction Audit
Risk Analysis Matrix

Name	*Partial general risks*	Group	*Sample Only*

ISSUE	Risk	PROCESS AND CONTROLS	AUDIT TEST
Section: Safety			
1. Unsafe Working Conditions	Accidental Death or Injury	Procedures include site safety regulations, training, site safety officer and periodic inspections.	1. Ensure procedures in place. 2. Review safety logs. 3. Perform walkthrough
2. Unsecured/Unsigned Perimeter Access	Accidental Injury to Bystanders	Signage around perimeter, gates around perimeter, locks and access control mechanisms are in place.	1. Observation of work site during working hours. 2. Observation of work site after working hours.
3. Unskilled/Untrained Workers	Substandard work resulting in dangerous conditions.	Require all workers to carry trade union cards or other proof or qualification during background employment checks.	1. Test for proof of training and requisite licenses.
4. Evacuation routes not part of design	Unable to safely evacuate building in an emergency	Plan and communicate evacuation routes. Require safety drills.	1. Ensure that evacuation routes have been planned and communicated. 2. Obtain results of last drill.
5. Improper equipment or use of safety apparel. (Unbalanced cranes)	Worker or bystander hurt due to worker negligence	Require use of safety equipment and provide backup safety equipment in case a worker reports without. Alternatively, require that employees be sent home without pay if they show up unprepared.	1. Observation of workers on site.
6. Safety log not maintained.	Root cause analysis cannot be performed and corrective action cannot be recommended.	Establish incident reporting standards and communicate to laborers at kick off meetings and with periodic reminders in their paychecks.	1. Obtain copy of safety log. 2. Review for repeat offenses. 3. Interview about follow up or contingencies to reduce future incidences.

Control Key Legend:
For each process step: V= Validity/Authorization Control C=Completeness Control A= Accuracy/Valuation Control P= Presentation/Classification Control
For the overall process: T= Timeliness/Efficiency Control SD= Segregation of Duties Control
For control weaknesses: MC= Missing/Weak Control

Figure 2.1 Construction audit risk analysis matrix.

Construction Audit
Risk Analysis Matrix

Name	*Partial general risks*	**Group**	*Sample Only*

7. Workers are intoxicated or under the influence of medications effecting judgment.	Judgment is impaired while using combustible or heavy equipment.	Mandatory drug or alcohol screening is included in labor contracts.	1. Look for signs of intoxication on employees. 2. Review safety logs for incidences caused by one or more repeat employees. 3. Perform surprise drug and alcohol screening.
8. Over-fatigued or dehydrated workers	Judgment is impaired while using combustible or heavy equipment	Procedures call for mandatory breaks and access to proper fluids and first aid as needed.	1. Observe work site and ensure workers are taking breaks. 2. Ensure that surplus fluids are available on site. 3. Identify first aid supplies. 4. Review procedures for first aid protocol. 5. Look for workers working excessive shifts or for more hours then local labor laws will allow.
9. Un-secured small or combustible materials.	In extreme weather conditions, small materials become dangerous flying objects, combustibles may ignite in extreme heat.	Lock up material and have proper sign in and inspection of material and combustibles.	1. Perform spot inspections. 2. Inspect to insure tools and combustibles are safely locked away.
10. Lack of incidence Response plan.	In case of accident, critical time may be lost in developing a response or treating an injured person.	Incidence response plan is in place and communicated to workers. Procedures are posted for easy reference.	1. Look for postings on site of incidence response plans. 2. Interview foremen and supervisors as to how to handle emergencies.

Control Key Legend:
For each process step: V= Validity/Authorization Control C=Completeness Control A= Accuracy/Valuation Control P= Presentation/Classification Control
For the overall process: T= Timeliness/Efficiency Control SD= Segregation of Duties Control
For control weaknesses: MC= Missing/Weak Control

Figure 2.1 (Continued)

Construction Audit
Risk Analysis Matrix

Name	Partial general risks	Group	Sample Only

Section: Cost			
1. Unsigned/Unsecured Perimeter Access	Theft of materials or dangerous equipment.	Procedures are in place to gate and lock the perimeter. Workers are easily identifiable and visitors are escorted.	1. Observation and site visit. 2. Reconciliation of physical and perpetual inventory records.
2. Budgets are not carefully planned.	Project costs are greater then what treasury or organization can handle or has anticipated.	Budgets are established and procedures are in place to reconcile and adjust budget as the project progresses. Budgets are on a system that allows for restricted access and audit trail. Budget status is addressed at weekly construction meetings.	1. Ensure budget is in place. Review for variances and obtain explanations for variances greater than 5%. 2. Interview Treasury personnel to ensure funding allocations are on track.
3. Invoices are paid without due diligence or proper documentation.	Payment for goods and services not received.	Procedures are in place to allow for open access to audit and for audit of invoices as they come in. Exceptions are noted and tracked.	1. Reconcile all invoices against backup provided. 2. Recalculate mathematics on all invoices. 3. Test approval of invoices against internal signing authorities.
4. Inferior work resulting in the need for redo.	Organization needs to pay out money to have substandard work corrected.	Lien waivers are received for all invoices. Architect who signs the lien waiver is independent in terms of fee and selection.	1. Verify there is no relationship between architect and vendors. 2. Examine contract of architect and ensure it is not based on overall construction spend. 3. Ensure that lien waivers are evidenced for all invoices prior to approval.

Control Key Legend:
For each process step: V= Validity/Authorization Control C=Completeness Control A= Accuracy/Valuation Control P= Presentation/Classification Control
For the overall process: T= Timeliness/Efficiency Control SD= Segregation of Duties Control
For control weaknesses: MC= Missing/Weak Control

Figure 2.1 (Continued)

Construction Audit
Risk Analysis Matrix

Name	Partial general risks	Group	Sample Only

5. Insurance not in place	Company cannot get compensated for claims due to catastrophic loss or injury.	Verification of insurance is done and property owner is listed as 'additional insured'.	1. Obtain copy of insurance policy. 2. Compare to contract requirements. 3. Call insurance company to verify that policy is in place.
6. Vendor's financial health was not verified prior to selection.	Vendor unable to complete job and new vendor must be selected resulting in lost time and additional costs.	Due diligence steps are clearly defined. and include Dunn and Bradstreet or audited financial statements.	1. Interview procurement personnel to determine what was done to get a qualified pool of vendors. 2. Audit compliance with internal policies.
7. Payments made before allowable.	Liquidity issues are faced within Treasury functions.	Documentation support for all invoices includes certification of completion verified by a skilled and independent party.	1. Reconcile payments to certification of completion from architect. 2. Ensure that budget amounts and percentages of completion are consistent from one month to the next (changes should be matched to approved change orders) 3. Talk to treasury and document any exception they have had with payments.
8. Vendor charges for employees who are not on site or are otherwise ghost employees.	Payment for services not received; increase risk of additional fraud.	Invoices are supported with certified payroll.	1. Surprise audit paycheck delivery. 2. Look for evidence of employees with inconsistent birthdates. 3. Look for employees with missing ID numbers or duplicate ID numbers.

Control Key Legend:
For each process step: V= Validity/Authorization Control C=Completeness Control A= Accuracy/Valuation Control P= Presentation/Classification Control
For the overall process: T= Timeliness/Efficiency Control SD= Segregation of Duties Control
For control weaknesses: MC= Missing/Weak Control

Figure 2.1 (Continued)

Construction Audit
Risk Analysis Matrix

Name	*Partial general risks*	Group	*Sample Only*

9. Right to audit does not exist in the contract.	Owner cannot verify costs incurred on the property and may not be able to classify costs correctly.	Contracts signed contain a Right to audit for a minimum of 3 years from completion of construction project.	1. Verify that a right to audit exists. 2. Document the expiration date of the clause
10. Right to scrap and salvage not specified in the contract.	Material bought by owner may be sold without financial benefit be giving to the proper owner.	Signed contracts are reviewed by legal and right to scrap and salvage clauses are included. Mitigating control – if costs call for reimbursement of "actual use" this is an alternate control for a right to scrap or salvage clause.	1. Verify that a right to scrap or salvage exists. 2. Test that a credit was received for the scrap and salvage
11. Project funding runs out	Solvency of project comes into questions or other projects are in jeopardy.	Budget Monitoring processes is in place and includes reporting to Treasury.	1. Inquire with treasury as to ability to pay for project. 2. Check progress of completion to the current amount spent and compare to budgeted spend. 3. Used earned value management tools to determine budget at completion.
12. Equipment is mishandled causing deposits made to be void.	Company does not receive full credit back on deposits..	Equipment is locked and stored nightly and operated only by licensed operators.	1. Visually inspect equipment and see how it is being handled. 2. Verify that operators have been trained for the equipment they are using.
13. Project is funded by restrictive donors, loans or foreign investors.	Investor or currency exchanger risk	Restricted funds are be classified separately and restrictions on those funds are considered during planning and project progress.	1. Identify any restrictions on funding sources. 2. Inquire with project manager as to how these restrictions are being considered and reported on during project progression.

Control Key Legend:
For each process step: V= Validity/Authorization Control C=Completeness Control A= Accuracy/Valuation Control P= Presentation/Classification Control
For the overall process: T= Timeliness/Efficiency Control SD= Segregation of Duties Control
For control weaknesses: MC= Missing/Weak Control

Figure 2.1 (Continued)

Construction Audit
Risk Analysis Matrix

Name	Partial general risks	Group	Sample Only

14. Lost of material, supplies or other small goods due to embezzlement or improper storage of same.	Payments for services that are lost or stolen.	Procedures are in place to ensure laborers return all materials, supplies and small goods to a locked shed or other secure facility before signing out for the day.	1. Review change order log for charges for lost items. 2. Reconcile a perpetual and physical inventory. 3. Inquire of procedures to sign in and out for small goods and equipment. 4. Modify audit to test compliance with these procedures.
15. Insufficient information to properly classify costs.	Costs may not be properly reflected on owner's financial statements.	Support for invoices contains enough information to determine where costs should be allocated to.	1. Examine documentation received with all invoices and test that costs are allocated to the correct trades.

Section: CHANGE MANAGEMENT			
1. Change orders are not approved but work is done.	Payment for goods or service not needed or wanted.	Procedures exist to sign and date approvals on change orders. Change orders submitted without approval are rejected for payment.	1. Test all change orders for approved signatures and signed approval.
2. Change orders submitted for items already included in scope or billed elsewhere on the project	Fraud; duplicate payment of goods/services received.	Change order requests are checked against original scope prior to approval.	1 Review change order log and compare sample to contract, noting any overlaps or suspicious requests.

Control Key Legend:
For each process step: V= Validity/Authorization Control C=Completeness Control A= Accuracy/Valuation Control P= Presentation/Classification Control
For the overall process: T= Timeliness/Efficiency Control SD= Segregation of Duties Control
For control weaknesses: MC= Missing/Weak Control

Figure 2.1 (Continued)

Construction Audit
Risk Analysis Matrix

Name	Partial general risks	Group	Sample Only
3. Change orders resulting in costs well in excess of budgeted costs.	Liquidity of project.	Budgets are updated on a regular basis and show estimated costs and impact of change orders approved.	1. Review current costs against original project budget and examine for unexplained variances.
4. Change orders put in for work not completed.	Payment for goods/service not received.	Documentation that work has been completed must be included with copy of approved change order. Change orders submitted without proof are rejected.	Verify change order log against change orders paid, specifically looking for change orders that were denied by owners.
5. Change approved without consideration for end use or effect on project.	Project does not function as needed or alternations above and beyond initial change must be made.	Clinical support or end user support signs off on requested change orders. Change order logs are distributed to end users at a regular frequency.	1. Inquire with end users as to effect change has on end use. 2. Ensure end user had knowledge of the change. 3. Look at change order log distribution reports.
6. Change submits to correct errors occurring from builder or architect.	Cost for change is inappropriately passed on to owner and accountability is not properly maintained.	Architect and builder are required to carry professional liability or errors and omissions insurance. Change orders resulting from architect error and submitting against architect's errors and omissions policy.	1. Verify the existence and validity of insurance policy. 2. Review change order log for changes that appear to be result of builder or architect error. Inquire as to why they were approved. 3. Review for any change orders denied as being architect or builder error – follow through to ensure these change orders were not subsequentially submitted for reimbursement.
7. Procedures are not clear as to how to	Owner pays more then anticipated or desired for change items. Timing or cost is	Change order procedures are included in construction manual or construction	1. Review contract or manual for inclusion of change order procedures.

Control Key Legend:
For each process step: V= Validity/Authorization Control C=Completeness Control A= Accuracy/Valuation Control P= Presentation/Classification Control
For the overall process: T= Timeliness/Efficiency Control SD= Segregation of Duties Control
For control weaknesses: MC= Missing/Weak Control

Figure 2.1 (Continued)

Construction Audit
Risk Analysis Matrix

Name	Partial general risks	Group	Sample Only
cost or submit change items.	compromised because clear directions for the submission of change items does not exist.	contract.	
8. Management approves changes not required for initial project.	Scope creep occurs.	Effective project governance is in place to allow open access to management and to communicate plans and progresses.	1. On a sample basis look at change order and examine end result to ensure project completion is within the parameters of initial plans.
9. Change orders are split so that they can get approved within signers limit.	Changes are approved without the necessary signing authority intended by management.	Authority limits are set consistent with job function. Change order logs are reviewed by upper management and discussed at routine construction meetings.	1. Review change order log and look for change orders submitted in sudden succession or for even amounts. If possible use data analytics to test change order log.
10. Change orders are not approved in a timely fashion.	Change orders awaiting approval delay project completion, increase chance of additional costs and may result in the need for overtime.	Procedures are in place to get change orders approved within a certain time and there are contingency plans in place when authorized signer is not available.	1. Analyze change order logs for change orders that are not approved within time parameters set in procedures. 2. Ensure that when signee is absent there are contingency plans
Section: QUALITY			
1. Substandard materials are used.	Quality of the project is compromised.	Materials of lading are received for all reimbursed material. Material invoices are compared to requirements established in the	1. Inquire with architect as to any problems with material. 2. Analyze change order log for replacement material requests,

Control Key Legend:
For each process step: V= Validity/Authorization Control C=Completeness Control A= Accuracy/Valuation Control P= Presentation/Classification Control
For the overall process: T= Timeliness/Efficiency Control SD= Segregation of Duties Control
For control weaknesses: MC= Missing/Weak Control

Figure 2.1 (Continued)

Construction Audit
Risk Analysis Matrix

Name	*Partial general risks*	Group	*Sample Only*

		architectural plans.	3. Verify a sample of material invoices back to architectural plans.
2. Unskilled or unqualified workers are used.	Improper construction methods compromise the overall structure built.	Hiring procedures include verification of experience and licenses.	1. Test a sample of laborers from certified payroll for correct license or training. 2. Review HR files and/or resumes to verify experience.
3. Geological factors not considered in planning phase.	Foundation or building methods used are not sufficient for the area in which the construction is done, potential code violation resulting in fines or failure to secure needed certifications.	Architect familiar with the area in which the construction is built assisted in original design. Soil testing was done to look for special conditions to be considered (oil, water, level of salt or sand)	1. If need be talk to a resident engineer or consulting engineer for a second opinion on how construction was handled. 2. Check with municipalities to see if any inspections turned up issues with construction. 3. Interview architect to see if any special factors were considered. 4. Look for soil testing results and question architect to see if he knows of the results.
4. Substandard work is done.	New vendors need to be called in to replace faulty construction.	Inspection are done at periodic basis (specifically behind the wall inspections) to test for quality and accuracy of construction methods used.	1. Review construction meetings looking for evidence from other parties that they were not satisfied with the results. 2. Check with municipalities to see if any inspections turned up issues with construction.
5. Materials do not perform to	Testing is not done during or after installation	Specialized material and construction	1. Inquire as to special

Control Key Legend:
For each process step: V= Validity/Authorization Control C=Completeness Control A= Accuracy/Valuation Control P= Presentation/Classification Control
For the overall process: T= Timeliness/Efficiency Control SD= Segregation of Duties Control
For control weaknesses: MC= Missing/Weak Control

Figure 2.1 (Continued)

Construction Audit
Risk Analysis Matrix

Name	*Partial general risks*	Group	*Sample Only*

specification.	of specialty construction.	methods are tested prior to implementation.	requirements needed for the project. 2. Obtain an explanation as t how the hurdles were overcome. 3. Obtain any test results done. 4. Determine any special treatment done to materials and their subsequent cost effect.
6. Architect is not independent of the contractor.	Work certified is not true, accurate, or free of conflict of interest. Bribery accepted to get substandard work passed through as satisfactory.	Architect's fees are not based on fee of the project. Architect holds required licensing. Background checks on architect's qualifications were done.	1. Perform check on architect to see if they are independent from a financial and a family perspective from the builder. 2. Document how the architect is paid. 3. Test to ensure that architect has signed all lien waivers.
7. Products are substituted for cheaper, alternative products.	Projects wishing to get special certifications, such as LEEDS standards, may be at risk of not obtaining desired assessment.	Materials of lading are received for all reimbursed material. Material invoices are compared to requirements established in the architectural plans.	1. Inquire with architect as to any problems with material. 2. Analyze change order log for replacement material requests, 3. Verify a sample of material invoices back to architectural plans. 4. If desired certification are not obtained, inquire as to why.
8. Warranties are not secured for products or fixtures used in the project.	Should problems arise after transfer of ownership, owner has no recourse to get product or fixture fixed, serviced, or replaced.	A final notebook containing samples, plans and final warranties is turned over prior to release of final funds and retainage.	1. Obtain copies of warranties obtained for fixtures and equipments. 2. Reconcile warranties to fixed assets.

Control Key Legend:
For each process step: V= Validity/Authorization Control C=Completeness Control A= Accuracy/Valuation Control P= Presentation/Classification Control
For the overall process: T= Timeliness/Efficiency Control SD= Segregation of Duties Control
For control weaknesses: MC= Missing/Weak Control

Figure 2.1 (Continued)

Construction Audit
Risk Analysis Matrix

Name	*Partial general risks*	**Group**	*Sample Only*

			3. Inquire as to any fixed assets without corresponding warranties.
9. Excessive repairs need to be made after owner moves in.	Excessive costs incurred to maintain facilities.	Guarantees of work quality is obtained for a period of 3–5 years post construction.	1. Interview end users at time of move in and then again 6 months later to assess satisfaction. 2. Obtain records of all repair costs and review for damages that appear outside normal wear and tear.
10. Quality exceeds the need of the project.	Costs are unnecessarily jeopardized or incurred beyond intentions of initial project.	Changes to the requirement of the project need to be approved by executive management.	1. Obtain change order log. 2. For work completed over initial scope inquire as to why approval was given.
Section: SCOPE			
1. Change orders submitted for items already in scope.	Payments for goods or services not needed,	Effective project governance is in place to allow open access to management and to communicate plans and progresses.	1. On a sample basis look at change order and examine end result to ensure project completion is within the parameters of initial plans.
2. Architect is unaware of owner's full intentions for the project.	Project is designed and does not fully meet the owner's requirements.	Communications to architect as to exact plans and specification are in writing and clearly defiend.	1. Interview end users and assess level of satisfaction to meet their needs. 2. Obtain a copy of original plans to architect and ensure intentions are clearly defined.

Control Key Legend:
For each process step: V= Validity/Authorization Control C=Completeness Control A= Accuracy/Valuation Control P= Presentation/Classification Control
For the overall process: T= Timeliness/Efficiency Control SD= Segregation of Duties Control
For control weaknesses: MC= Missing/Weak Control

Figure 2.1 (Continued)

Construction Audit
Risk Analysis Matrix

Name	*Partial general risks*	Group	*Sample Only*

3. Builder does not build to architects specifications.	Project is completed and does not fully meet the owner's requirements.	Architect signs off on work completed by builder. Builder and architect meet weekly to discuss progress, status and next steps. Minutes of the meeting are recorded and distributed.	1. Interview architect and determine any problems they had with the builder. 2. Obtain a copy of the meeting minutes and review for discrepancies not resolved.
4. Vendor does not perform all duties required of them. (securing permits)	Project is at jeopardy because key steps are eliminated, missed or otherwise not completed.	Responsibilities of the vendors are clearly defined in the contract. Project governance procedures are in place to test vendor compliance with contract requirements.	1. Obtain contract and highlight responsibilities of the vendors. 2. Test compliance with responsibilities including: ■ Obtaining insurance ■ Paying deposits or down payments ■ Invoice Submission procedures ■ Securing approvals
5. Responsibilities of vendors overlap.	Payment for services not needed and duplication of efforts.	Responsibilities of vendors are clearly defined in the contract and are consistent with scope.	1. Review contracts and map out responsibility of key vendors. 2. Examine responsibility for segregation of duties, overlap, or responsibilities outside the expertise of the vendor.
6. Scope of services not clearly defined in the contract.	Services not delivered as anticipated or expected.	Contract includes clear, concise text outlining scope of contract.	1. Review contract and outline scope of contract. 2. Ensure scope is consistent with expertise of the vendor.

Control Key Legend:
For each process step: V= Validity/Authorization Control C=Completeness Control A= Accuracy/Valuation Control P= Presentation/Classification Control
For the overall process: T= Timeliness/Efficiency Control SD= Segregation of Duties Control
For control weaknesses: MC= Missing/Weak Control

Figure 2.1 (Continued)

Construction Audit
Risk Analysis Matrix

Name	*Partial general risks*	Group	*Sample Only*

7. Scope short-cutted to save time and money without the knowledge of the owner.	Payment for goods and service not received as well as potential compromised quality	Independent, qualified third party should certify work done. Behind the wall inspections should be done quickly. Contract calls for notification to architect or project manager before sealing walls or ceilings.	1. Obtain inspections done to test for compliance with behind the wall work. 2. Document that lien waivers were received and signed by an independent third party. 3. Verify credentials of partying signing off on lien waivers. 4. Identify clause in contract that calls for inspections and notifications before sealing walls and ceilings.
8. Performance bond not secured or bond presented is fraudulent	Claims for performance bonds or bid bonds are nullified or disqualified.	Bonds should be obtained and secured with a surety company acceptable by property owners.	1. Obtain Contract requirements for bonds. 2. Discuss with Risk Manager acceptability of surety companies. 3. Call surety company and validate bond is true and in effect.
9. Scope is not clearly defined in bid packages.	Prices received back on bids is inadequate and may result in excess change orders or costs/timing in excess of what is bid.	Scope on RFP should be clear and accurately reflect the needs of the end project.	1. Identify scope in RFPs. 2. Compare bid packages to RFPs and ensure winning vendor met all requirements in the RFP. 3. Compare change orders back to RFP to see if it was part of originally bid scope.
10. Scope changes after initial planning designs are made can be more costly.	Increased risk of cost overruns.	Plans should be spelled out prior to work completed.	1. Document planning process 2. Identify and scope changes made after construction were

Control Key Legend:
For each process step: V= Validity/Authorization Control C=Completeness Control A= Accuracy/Valuation Control P= Presentation/Classification Control
For the overall process: T= Timeliness/Efficiency Control SD= Segregation of Duties Control
For control weaknesses: MC= Missing/Weak Control

Figure 2.1 (Continued)

Construction Audit
Risk Analysis Matrix

Name	*Partial general risks*	**Group**	*Sample Only*

			done. 3. Evaluate impact of change on project.
Section: FUNCTION			
1. Needs of end users are not considered during planning.	Rework may be necessary to meet the needs of end users.	End user acceptance and interviews should be done as part of the planning process.	1. Determine and document planning process.
2. Changes/Plans made result in unusable space.	Effect on project may domino to other users.	End user and IT support should be obtained while approving and managing change orders.	Document change management function.
3. Planning does not consider needs of future expansion/business growth.	Space utilization cannot be optimized and may result in the need for future building/construction before intended.	Floor plan should be based on current needs as well as anticipated growth.	Obtain original planning documents and determine that future growth has been considered.
4. Project is over-customized and future resale of use of the project is limited.	Conversion opportunity or cost of the project is compromised in the future.	Plans should be generic enough to meet needs of end users and customizations should be appropriate to meet corporate culture, philosophy and policies.	1. Observe any portions of the scope that may seem overly modern or customized. 2. Look at key stakeholders and project influencers and ensure that personal offices are done according to company standards.
5. Design plans violate regulatory requirements.	Rework necessary to bring building up to code or forfeiture of use may be required.	A licensed and local architect or engineer should be used to review plans for code compliance. Regulatory permits are filed	1. Ensure a review by a licensed professional was done. 2. Determine that professional

Control Key Legend:
For each process step: V= Validity/Authorization Control C=Completeness Control A= Accuracy/Valuation Control P= Presentation/Classification Control
For the overall process: T= Timeliness/Efficiency Control SD= Segregation of Duties Control
For control weaknesses: MC= Missing/Weak Control

Figure 2.1 (Continued)

Construction Audit
Risk Analysis Matrix

Name	Partial general risks	Group	*Sample Only*

		for and include copies of planning documents.	has local experience and experience in the type of project completed. 3. Obtain copies of permits. 4. Discuss any possible violations or problems with municipal authorities (website search may be available depending on locality).
6. Project is completed but does not meet the needs or adaptability to utility suppliers.	Project cannot be used as required because requisite water, power, or electricity needs cannot be met.	Utility company should be consulted in planning phase.	1. Ensure a review by a licensed professional was done. 2. Obtain copies of permits. Discuss any possible violations or problems with municipal / utility authorities (website search may be available depending on locality).
7. Communication protocols are not sufficient for key decision makers to make informed decisions about the project.	Decisions made using poor information result in inability to use the project as intended or result in rework/return of goods.	Established communication protocols and reports needs to be established with key stakeholders and decisions makers and changes, statuses and reports needs to be delivered at timely intervals.	1. Document communication protocols and determine that key stakeholders are giving information they need to make informed decisions.
8. Overall project design is disturbing to 'neignbors.'	Projects may be stopped or the reputation of the project is harmed when surrounding neighbors cause a disturbance.	Project curfew is established.	Review sign in sheets or time cards to ensure no work is being done after established hours.

Control Key Legend:
For each process step: V= Validity/Authorization Control C=Completeness Control A= Accuracy/Valuation Control P= Presentation/Classification Control
For the overall process: T= Timeliness/Efficiency Control SD= Segregation of Duties Control
For control weaknesses: MC= Missing/Weak Control

Figure 2.1 (Continued)

Construction Audit
Risk Analysis Matrix

Name	*Partial general risks*	**Group**	*Sample Only*

Section: TIMING			
1. Unexpected weather conditions cause work stoppage.	Project not completed on time or overtime required to finish on schedule.	• Schedule includes a buffer for normal weather patterns. • Procedures are in place to monitor for weather emergencies.	• Inquire as to procedures for weather delays. • Summarize change orders for timing due to weather.
2. Long lead time items or other material needs not ordered.	Construction delayed waiting for the needs of equipment.	Long lead time items ordered in advance	Document any delays due to lack of material or equipment.
3. Discovery of archeological remains or crime scenes.	Projects may be halted until experts can remove remains and allow construction to commence.	Delays due to archaeological findings must be reported as soon as remains are found. Historical research was carried out.	Document any delays due to site being shut for removal of artifacts. Observe copies of historical research.

Control Key Legend:
For each process step: V= Validity/Authorization Control C=Completeness Control A= Accuracy/Valuation Control P= Presentation/Classification Control
For the overall process: T= Timeliness/Efficiency Control SD= Segregation of Duties Control
For control weaknesses: MC= Missing/Weak Control

Figure 2.1 (Continued)

NOTES

1 Ukconstructionmedia.co.uk, Seven Reasons why 69% of Construction Projects exceed their budgets.
2 Manhattanda.org, *Construction Management Executive Robert Baselice Allegedly Led Conspiracy that Stole Millions from Developers, November 15, 2023.*
3 Burjkhalifa.ae.
4 FAA Title 14 CFR Part 77 (https://www.ecfr.gov/current/title-14/chapter-I/subchapter-E/part-77).
5 Copper Price Live|Copper Price Today|Copper Price Chart|IFCM UK.
6 Types of Theft That Affect the Construction Businesses (chron.com).

Chapter 3

How construction audit is different from other audits

Unlike other typical audits, such as process audits, business line audits, compliance audits, etc., a construction audit is a myriad of all the other types. It is a process audit, a contract audit and a compliance audit, all rolled into one. There are approximately 45 processes in the construction life cycle that can be audited individually or en masse. Figure 3.1 shows this.

There may be more or fewer processes depending on the organization and the type of construction. For example, when working with airports, the vendor selection process may contain fewer steps as they may have vendors already in place.

In the oil and gas industry, there will be additional steps such as exploration, special material handling and turnaround contracts. Also, the construction may be just part of a larger project and there will be more processes to integrate or complete the other parts of the project. One will need to decide if they want a full project audit or just an audit of construction activity.

Some construction audits are special requests of management, and they are not part of the audit lifecycle. In these cases, management may carve out which parts of the process will be audited.

As part of the audit process, the reporting process may be different than with traditional auditing. Sometimes the audit communications are less formal and may be just a memo to management. It is also possible that the audit is being done due to known overpayments and the results of the audit will go straight to the legal department. It is best to figure this out at the beginning.

Audit results may be used in potential lawsuits. Auditors should be carefully coached and trained as to how to report in this way. Legal should brief auditors on evidence, confidentiality and discovery (when the opposing party can get evidence in advance of trial) and should protect audit communications. They can do this by establishing 'Attorney-client privileges.' Audit should be reminded that they cannot start attorney-client privilege and it must be started by the legal team.

DOI: 10.1201/9781003461487-4

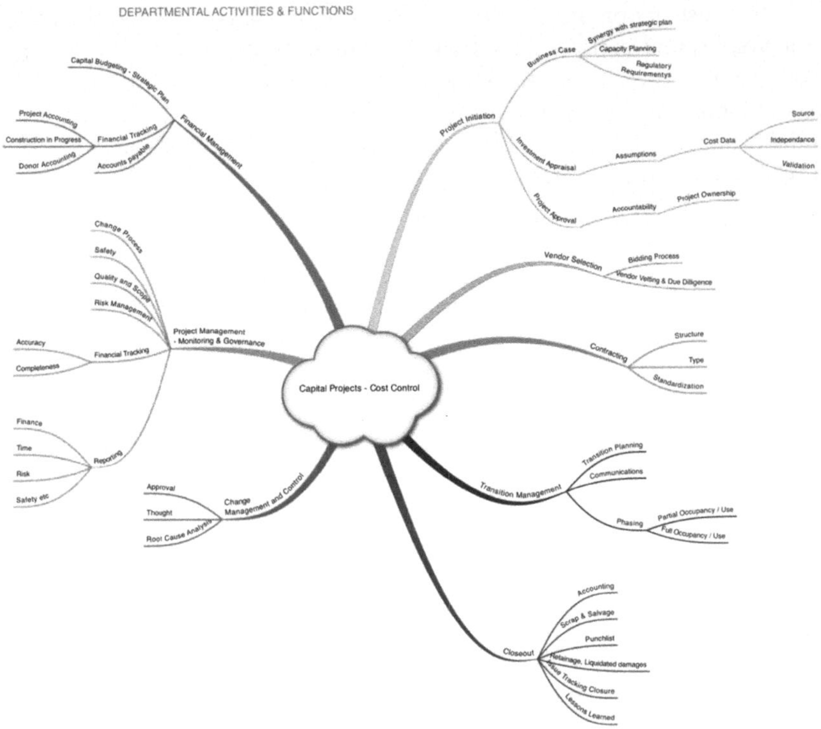

Figure 3.1 Processes involved in construction audit.

A construction audit and a traditional audit have different focuses and scopes. Traditional audit techniques include vouching, reconciling, verification, casting, analyzing and tallying. While some parts of construction audit rely on these tools, construction audit is an analysis of the costs and activities around the entire construction project and process. It includes tasks that you see in traditional audits, tools used by project management and sometimes an element of creativity. In a construction audit you are technically analyzing the contracts and processes, verifying and recalculating costs, prices and overhead, understanding reimbursements and forensically analyzing reimbursements. It is more than just the financial aspects as during the audit you may be called upon to assess project completeness, project communications, safety and other areas of the project.

While traditional audits typically focus on compliance with standards and financial integrity and accuracy, construction audits are more specific and focus on the costs and performance of the project.

With construction audit, you look at more population testing than with individual samples. If you relied on sampling in construction audit, you are likely to miss the whole picture. For example, when looking at invoices, if you audit an invoice by itself, you will likely miss certain things: duplicate reimbursements and change order submission. You want to see how invoices flow from one to the other.

Chapter 4

Delivering a construction audit

Delivering a construction audit effectively requires careful planning, organization and attention to detail. Here are some key steps the audit manager, or leader, can take to properly manage a construction audit:

1. *Determine the timing* – There are three approaches you can take when it comes to planning the audit. There is point in time, this is when you audit a given milestone, after construction and being an integral part of the construction team. Each comes with its own advantages and disadvantages as shown in Table 4.1.
2. *Define the audit objectives* – As we have mentioned, there are many areas of a construction project that can be audited. It is imperative that the objectives of the audit, such as verifying compliance with contractual agreements, assessing cost controls, evaluating quality standards, or identifying potential fraud or misuse of funds, are outlined and clearly communicated to the audit team. The scope can be extensive or narrowly focused depending on the assessed risks and available resources. Additionally, reports may be formal or informational updates/presentations. Report findings should be discussed with the client (typically the project team and the executive sponsor). If you wait until a project is done, some findings may be 'too little, too late.' This requires that significant findings are reported on a quicker, more informal basis. This is especially true when identifying overpayments/overcharges.
3. *Assemble an audit team* – Form a competent and independent audit team consisting of professionals with relevant expertise, such as construction project managers, accountants, engineers and legal experts. You can either train a construction professional how to audit or train an auditor about construction. I 'fell' into it as I knew the property where renovations were being done, as I had audited the property in the past. Ensure that the team members have a clear understanding of the audit objectives and their roles in the process. Try to partner auditors up if they are new to construction audit so they can learn and develop professionally.

DOI: 10.1201/9781003461487-5

Table 4.1 When should construction audit take place?

Point in time	*After construction*	*Integral part of construction team*
Definition		
Auditor performs an audit as certain milestones are reached or audits a set of payments at a time.	Auditor waits until the project is over before the audit starts.	Auditor sits as a non-voting member of the construction team and audits the project as it commences.
Advantages		
Auditor has access to all the construction team.	Auditor does not get in the way.	Auditor can observe rather than relying on the memory of others.
Findings or control weaknesses can be rectified before the problem escalates.	It is easier for the audit to evaluate the 'big picture.'	Findings or control weaknesses can be rectified before the problem escalates.
Less strain on audit resources, as the audit can be done in small pieces.	Invoice issues may be more evident if they are audited as a group.	Easier to obtain necessary documents and backup.
	It is easier for an audit to divide the work between a team of auditors.	There are no continuity issues if the same auditor is used.
Easier to organize.		Easier to organize.
		More access to construction team can result in better auditor/auditee relationships.
Audit has direct knowledge and observation.		Audit has direct knowledge and observation.
Disadvantages		
		Long commitment of a single auditor and project may be difficult to pass on to other auditors.
Billing issues may be harder to detect.		Billing issues may be harder to detect.
Auditor may seem to get in the way or impede progress.	Auditor has to rely on the memory of the construction team, who may or may not be available to talk to.	Auditor may seem to get in the way or impede progress.
	Findings have escalated and the organization loses out on interest or other uses of the funds.	If an auditor should leave the organization, the audit of the project may face continuity issues.

(*Continued*)

Table 4.1 (Continued)

Point in time	*After construction*	*Integral part of construction team*
If too many issues arise, audit may be accused of 'witch hunting.'	Audit may take longer to look over the whole project at once.	If too many issues arise, audit may be accused of 'witch hunting.'
	Documents may have been lost, destroyed, or missing.	Auditor has to audit backward with available paperwork and access to external members of the team is not readily available.
	There is a risk that audit rights have expired.	
Unless the same auditor is used, continuity issues will prevail.		

Often, during a construction audit, you will have to be assertive with members of management. Choose teammates who can do that without being unprofessional or without getting intimidated. You want to consider putting someone who is adept with financial forensics on the team. Many payments go through certain layers and the money will need to be traced forward or backwards to get the true value. Someone comfortable with spreadsheets can come in handy.

4. *Develop an audit plan* – Prepare a comprehensive audit plan outlining the scope, methodology and timeline of the audit. The plan should identify the key areas to be audited, the audit procedures to be followed and the resources required. It should also include provisions for addressing any potential risks or challenges that may arise during the audit. When staff does not have the requisite experience, I have seen where the audit kick-off meeting and a training session have been done simultaneously. This allows the audit team to use their new skills right away and apply what they learned in class.
5. *Conduct a preliminary review* – Before initiating the audit, perform a preliminary review of relevant documentation, contracts, project plans, financial records and other relevant materials. This will help identify areas of potential concern or focus for the audit team and provide a foundation for the audit process. In some cases, it may also spell out if the organization even has the right to audit the general contractor and the subsidiaries. The contract may spell out the limits of the review either by time limits (you can normally look back three years) or limit what can be examined (you may not have access to payroll records).

6. *Prepare the auditors* – This may be unchartered territory for auditors. They should be trained as to their expectation and the tools that they can access to do the review. There should also be specific rules as to whether auditors will need to go on-site, and if so, which auditors. Auditors who need to go on-site should undergo additional training. There is a 10-hour Construction Site Safety course with the Occupational Safety and Health Administration, aka OSHA. Information and enrolment can be found on the OSHA website at www.osha.gov. Workers chosen to go on-site will also need well-fitted protective equipment (hard hats, special shoes), allows them have enough time to get the equipment if necessary.
7. *Execute the audit* – Carry out the audit procedures as outlined in the audit plan. This may involve conducting site visits, interviewing project personnel, reviewing financial records, inspecting construction progress and comparing actual costs with budgeted amounts.

   Ensure that the audit team follows proper documentation and record-keeping practices throughout the process. Because there is so much to look at, you may roll out the audit in phases and the reporting may also be done in phases. This is where the informal reporting process may be a more judicious course than a formal report. If auditor will roll on and off the construction audit, there should be at least one person who is on the team as a central person, just to ensure that information and communication remain open.
8. *Monitor progress* – Regularly monitor the progress of the audit to ensure that it is on track and aligned with the established objectives and timeline. Maintain open communication with the audit team to address any issues, challenges or questions that may arise during the audit. Many of the audit steps are observational and may require attending and observing construction meetings. Keep in mind that this will interfere with the speed of audit progress and should not be help against the auditors. If you hold it against the auditors, they may rush through other steps or take shortcuts that will impede overall audit results.
9. *Analyze findings* – Once the audit fieldwork is complete, the audit team should analyze the findings and observations. Should there be a finding about overpayments, a review should be done to identify the 'true' amount of the finding. Additionally, the vendor may need to be reported to Purchasing, especially if there are many repeat issues. As we will discuss when talking about auditing payments, there are adjustments that need to be made.

   Identify any instances of non-compliance, deviations from standards or potential irregularities. This analysis should be based on objective evidence and supported by appropriate documentation. Look for any cause and event scenarios to see if additional testing may be needed.

   All or some findings may need to be rolled to other departments.

10. *Prepare the audit report* – Compile the audit findings, conclusions and recommendations into a comprehensive audit report. The report should clearly communicate the audit results, highlighting areas of concern, suggesting improvements and providing actionable recommendations. It should be concise, well-structured and supported by relevant evidence.

    The audit report, however, may not be like normal audit reports, as the report may be an interim report if the project is still ongoing. Many times, in construction audit, management may want touchpoints along the way to ensure progress is being made as planned.

    It is not recommended when doing an interim review to wait until the project ends as it may not be over for several years. It is better to correct the issues as soon as they are found. In these cases, memo-format audit reports may be used. It is important to discuss how reporting will be done early in the process.
11. *Communicate the results* – Present the audit report to the relevant stakeholders, including senior management, project owners or regulatory authorities. Clearly communicate the audit findings, explaining the implications and significance of each observation. Ensure that any sensitive or confidential information is appropriately handled and shared only with authorized individuals. Audit should be aware of what, if any, issues should be sent to other areas, such as Legal or in some cases, Treasury Management or Risk Management.
12. *Follow-up and implementation* – Track the implementation of audit recommendations and corrective actions based on the audit findings. Regularly assess the progress made in addressing the identified issues. Monitor the effectiveness of the corrective measures and provide necessary support to ensure compliance and improvement.

By following these steps, a manager can effectively manage a construction audit, ensuring thoroughness, objectivity and adherence to professional standards.

AN ALTERNATE APPROACH

Normally, construction audits are done on a project-by-project basis and many issues can be found. However, if multiple projects are being done, an alternate approach should be adopted. There should still be project-by-project audits; however, additional vendor audits should be done. This is a more practical way to discover:

- Duplicate billings – using one item and charging it to multiple projects.
- Misallocation of costs – applying costs of one project to another project. This is particularly risky when one project is a fixed fee, and the other is a cost-plus.

- Misallocated personnel costs – a worker works on one project and is reimbursed via another. This will normally be seen when a cost-plus contract is reaching its limit and the company still wants to get reimbursed for a worker. They may reimburse it via a newer project that is not yet at its limit. It may also be done to 'prove' a worker was due overtime.
- Discovery of supplier performance issues – a contractor may be having issues with a vendor, and it is mismanaged. Chances are problems will be symptomatic over the whole relationship and it will not be picked up by just looking at a single project at a time.
- Missing equipment – equipment that is missing on a project may not be missing at all, it is simply being placed with the equipment of another project.

Your approach will be based on what your team had agreed to with executive management and possibly suspicions or findings from project-by-project audits.

Chapter 5

Pillars of success

So, what makes a successful project? It has to meet executive expectations and deliver on what is promised during the initial project appraisal. This can generally be broken down into six areas, which I term pillars of success.

1. Cost – The total cost of the project comes in on budget, under budget, or at a cost variance within an acceptable parameter. Auditors sometimes make the mistake of assuming cost is the priority but for many projects cost considerations are secondary or even tertiary. Though we call these pillars of success, one pillar or the action of that pillar may cause an action on another pillar.
2. Time – The project is finished on time. Projects that focus on time may be looking at opportunity costs such as the ability to generate revenue from the project. Consider if you are building a new casino/hotel on the Las Vegas strips, being late by three days can cost millions or more, not to mention any lost loyalty when guests who had reserved show up and you have no room for them. Often deadlines need to be adhered to and there is nothing that can be done to change the deadline.

   Assume that the project is to construct the Olympic Village for the Olympic Games; the stadium you are doing must be done in time for the opening ceremonies, there is no extension possible.

   As I write this book, I have noticed a new, luxury supermarket being built near my house. The store is coming together rather quickly and the holidays are quickly upon us. The sooner the supermarket can open, the sooner they can take advantage of the holiday rush and recover some of their construction costs. If they wait until after the holidays it will take considerably longer.
3. Safety – If no one goes home hurt or injured, then Safety has been maintained. Construction projects pose a big risk to safety due to the nature of construction activities. Popular areas of safety risk are trips and falls and crane collapses. Construction projects need to focus

DOI: 10.1201/9781003461487-6

on the safety of construction workers, neighbors, passersby and end users. We will look at how to prevent incidents and what to do once incidents occur in Chapter 28. Besides, accidents often cause financial loss and reputational damage. Compensation paid to injured workers can be considerable. An illustration of reputational risk is the World Cup in Qatar – the international press criticized certain aspects of safety.

4. Quality – Quality risk may be assigned to the 'pieces' used in construction or they can relate to the overall quality of the finished product. Sometimes with quality we see such things as the grade of finishes or the 'green-ness' of the end project. To be a quality construction building must, at a minimum, comply with local code. To an owner, they may want something that exceeds code. This comes at a cost, so owners should develop and communicate the criteria they are willing to accept.
5. Function – The project should be done if a business benefit could be recognized. The question to ask is, does the project deliver the benefit it set out to provide? To understand what the benefit was, you may need to review the project charter.
6. Scope – Getting what you need is nearly always the priority, regardless of the price. This is generally seen in projects that are being done for regulatory or special purposes. Scope needs to be communicated and clear for this pillar to be recognized. If your project is significantly over budget a decision to reduce scope or substitute inferior materials may be made. Consider if the goal is to build the tallest building in the world; if you build something with 86 floors, you will not achieve your scope goal.

   There are situations where circumstances change and the need for the project will change. Take for example, after Covid, many office buildings were left vacant – they were no longer needed as employees worked from home. If a project were to start on building a new headquarters, executive management may change their mind. For corporate offices, Human Resources should be part of the planning process, as they will know approximate censuses once the construction is completed. On other projects, anticipating future needs is also necessary; on the Central Artery Tunnel project they needed to predict future traffic patterns in the design of the new roads.

All these pillars are interrelated. If you cut scope, you may be cutting cost. If you are running short of time, you may implement overtime, which in turn increases cost. So, while it may be easy to think of each one as is, you need to consider the six pillars as a whole (Figure 5.1).

Figure 5.1 Pillars of project success.

Chapter 6

Phases of construction projects

There are seven major phases of construction, and each comes with different risks and different benefits (Figure 6.1). The major phases of construction are:

- Project Appraisal
- Project Initiation, also known as Project Conception.
- Pre-Construction
- Project Execution
- Commissioning
- Occupancy and Move In
- Closure

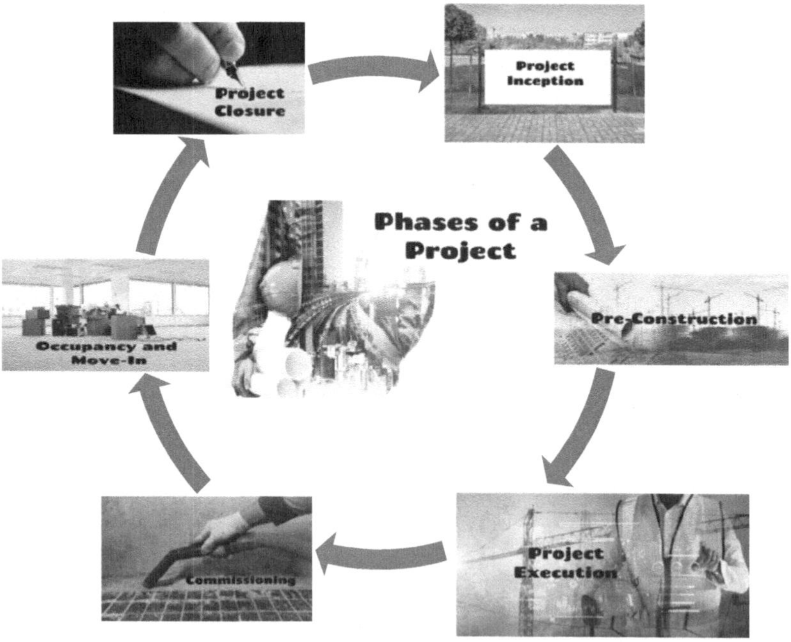

Figure 6.1 Phases of a project.

DOI: 10.1201/9781003461487-7

It is important for the auditor to properly identify what stage the project is at and to identify the same in the audit report. As we mentioned in risk, each phase brings about new risks and without knowing where the project is, the auditor will not be able to properly plan or prioritize steps for the audit.

PROJECT APPRAISAL

Project appraisal is the stage of the project where estimates of costs are made, a description of the project is formulated, and any information that the executive committee needs is drafted.

Project descriptions are spelled out along with strategic missions. In this phase, the project goes off to the executive team for approval. The team approves it, postpones it, asks for modifications or denies it. For this reason, it is possible that this is where the project ends, as well. When auditing the project appraisal process, auditors should find out controls to ensure rejected projects are not resubmitted after rejection. In some organizations that might allow resubmission.

PROJECT INITIATION OR PROJECT CONCEPTION

The difficult decisions have been made; the executive board has signed off on it. So, what comes next? Next, the parameters of the project are set up. We will call this Project Initiation Part 2. A lot of the Project Management literature often falls short of discussing this as a formal phase, but from an audit standpoint, it should not be overlooked. What happens during this phase is that the project (plus any special requirements of the executive board) is determined. A feasibility study may be done to see how realistic these parameters are.

Look at the Burj Khalifa. In 2010, the Burj Khalifa became the tallest building in the world at 2,717 feet.[1] Besides being the tallest building, Burj Khalifa is (has):

- The tallest free-standing structure in the world
- Highest number of stories in the world
- Highest occupied floor in the world
- Highest outdoor observation deck in the world
- Elevator with the longest travel distance in the world
- Tallest service elevator in the world

These are not records set by coincidence; these were by design. It came at a gamble, but before designing the building they had to determine that these designs could be done. Was it even possible? If it was possible, at what cost?

Can it be done with the extreme climate of Dubai? Would people feel comfortable at Burj Khalifa? All these questions and more had to be answered in the design phase and continued all the way through the construction.

Many people often confuse feasibility studies as solely determining whether a project can be done. But it goes further than that. It is to determine that a project can be done within the constraints enabled. Can it be done in the timeframe established? Who will be involved? Can it legally be done in the area desired (i.e., Casinos cannot be built just anywhere)? What goals should the project achieve?

During this phase you may even see business plans and grant applications. This should be collected by audit, as it will be referred to later. Also, at this point an auditor should determine how the project is being funded.

FOLLOW THE FUNDS!

As part of the audit, auditors should find out where the funds are coming from. Auditors play a crucial role in examining and validating the financial information of an organization to ensure accuracy, transparency, and compliance with relevant regulations. Understanding the funding sources for construction projects is important for auditors for several reasons:

1. **Compliance and Legal Requirements:** Auditors need to ensure that the organization complies with legal and regulatory requirements regarding the funding of capital projects. Different funding sources may come with specific rules and restrictions, and auditors must verify that these rules are followed to avoid legal and regulatory issues.
2. **Financial Reporting Accuracy:** Knowing the funding sources helps auditors ensure the accuracy of financial reporting. It allows them to verify that the financial statements properly reflect the sources of funds used for projects. This is essential for presenting a true and fair view of the organization's financial position.
3. **Risk Assessment:** Understanding the funding sources assists auditors in assessing the risks associated with capital projects. Different sources of funding may introduce varying degrees of risk, such as interest rate risk, repayment terms, or covenants. Auditors need to evaluate and consider these factors while doing their risk assessment on the project. For example, if funding is coming from sponsorships, they will need to know if donors have placed any restrictive covenants in place.
4. **Fraud Prevention:** Knowledge of funding sources helps auditors in detecting and preventing fraud. By understanding how funds are obtained and utilized, auditors can identify any irregularities or discrepancies that may indicate fraudulent activities, such as misappropriation of funds, conflicts of interest or unauthorized use of resources.

5. **Budgetary Control:** Auditors may assess whether the organization's budgetary control mechanisms are effective in managing capital project funds. They want to ensure that the organization allocates and uses funds for their intended purposes and that there are adequate controls in place to prevent misuse.
6. **Stakeholder Assurance:** Auditors may need to provide assurance to various stakeholders, including investors, lenders and regulatory bodies. Understanding the funding sources for projects allows auditors to communicate effectively with stakeholders and creditors.

In summary, auditors want to know about funding sources for construction projects to ensure compliance, verify financial reporting accuracy, assess risks, prevent fraud, evaluate budgetary control and provide assurance to stakeholders. This knowledge enables auditors to fulfill their responsibilities in conducting thorough and effective audits.

Funding sources can vary. Loans are usually the most common. This would be where the owner gets money traditionally, getting a construction or bridge loan with their bank. In some cases, the organization may have a pool of funds available to them. In other traditional financing arrangements, the owner may be able to 'draw' down money, when needed. This arrangement often comes with restrictions. It may even call for audits to be done.

There are times when the organization will receive an incentive to build in a particular area. Tax breaks are the most common incentive given. Even in this arrangement, restrictions may apply. Commonly we see restrictions such as using local labor or Minority and Women-Owned Business Enterprises (MWBEs). Care should be exercised as we often see MWBE fraud on construction projects. Mitigating the risk of MWBE fraud involves implementing robust processes and controls to ensure transparency, accountability and compliance. Audit should perform an audit of MWBE companies to ensure they are present and legitimate. A sample MWBE Audit is presented in the Building Your Construction Team chapter.

Another common source of funds is grants or bonds. The auditor's role includes understanding the terms and using that understanding while developing their risk matrix. Using bonds or grants can pose significant risks in the areas of financial management, compliance, reporting and project management. If terms are not complied with, funding may stop, regardless of the progress of the project. Auditor will need to ensure that their audit ensures that expenses are valid and in compliance with the contract. Failure to do so may result in funding being stopped. Be particularly careful if government funds are in use. In such instances, you may need to follow Federal Acquisitions Regulation (FAR) guidelines in the procurement of team members. FAR is the principal set of rules that governs the acquisition process of the federal government.

Audit will want to ensure that document guidelines are in place and complied with on the project. If external sources want to audit the project, it is important to know that the organization will be ready and can comply with these requests. This includes contracts, invoices, timecards, bidding documentation and other critical processes. Audit will need to ensure transparency in reporting to stakeholders and reporting requirements spelled out in the grant or bond agreements. By addressing these aspects, auditors will contribute to effective and responsible management of funds and relationships with funders. They will help foster transparency and mitigate potential risks.

PRE-CONSTRUCTION

The pre-construction phase is when important decisions are made for the project. Specifically, the team is 'built' and roles will be assigned for internal assignments versus external assignments. Important decisions have to be made to build the team, decide what roles all members will be assigned, and plan and sign contracts. The pre-construction phase includes creating a strategic plan for the project, creating a design, securing permits or entitlements, and gathering the labor and resources required for construction. Pre-construction services can provide owners with a formal approach for developing cost, scope and schedule to execute the construction on time and in control. There should be a discussion about feasibility.

The first thing discussed during pre-construction should be to define the project, define project requirements and define parameters. The more definition you give the project, the better you will be able to control the project. Hopefully the better-designed project will result in a deduction in change orders. Part of the constraints will be how much you want in contingency. Contingency is a 'budget' for going over budget. This amount is set internally so as to separate out what was committed and what was paid. Most projects will go over budget solely due to the fact that the plan did not go into enough detail.

Ideally contingency should be kept in a separate accounting code. The architect or architect/engineer will ask for this amount. I do not recommend disclosing it. If you do, likely they will see overcharges as allowable if they fit into this amount. You have more control if the amount is not disclosed.

Other things to design during pre-construction are to identify project milestones or touchpoints as to when your project lead needs to check in with the owners. The check-in phase is a lot easier to manage and maintain when you can see the site, when construction is remote to the owner, one needs to rely on what the contractor tells them. There should be compensating controls in place to ensure that the contractor is telling the truth. The most popular compensating control is cameras. There was a recent example of a hospital that was under construction. The contractor had been reporting on the status and accordingly said the project was on schedule. When the owners went to the project (to get ready for the grand opening), they saw that the demolition phase still had not been done, despite what the contractor said.

A plan needs to be agreed upon for. The project manager or contractor will need to share updates, statuses, problems and/or safety incidences. Who should these be sent to? How will they be sent? How will they be stored? Keep in mind that for safety incidences procedures need to be detailed out, however, when sharing incidences, that may mention a person or reveal a medical condition, it is important to maintain privacy and discretion. How long will you store the information that is shared? Additionally what information will you store? Documents may be created by audit – such as workpapers and interview notes or created by the contractor – such as invoices and Daily Foreman reports.

Early in the process, audit needs a method to accumulate these records and keep them in an accessible manner for all members of the audit team. It may be that Audit should call in expertise from Information technology or Information technology audit to ensure that the information is secure. Talking to Legal or Records Management may need to be done. Generally, the rules are that all documents related to construction of an asset need to be maintained for the life of the asset plus 13 years. This may vary in some jurisdictions but it is worth looking into.

Other documents that may be acquired are site photographs, safety incidence reports and minutes of the monthly construction meetings. Caution must be considered when contracting. Many contracts say that the auditors can request 'reasonably necessary documentation.' This is a problem; as reasonably necessary documentation is not defined anywhere, and the reasonably will be dependent on the audit scope. The contractor may find the request to be unreasonable.

It is often assumed that the audit scope is to verify the financial accuracy of the project. In many cases, however, the scope is much more involved. It is sometimes advisable to discuss this during the contract phases, but often there is so much going on that audit rights are placed on the back burner, only to emerge once it is too late.

During the project pre-construction phase a risk register should be completed and designed. It should indicate what anticipated hurdles may arise and any contingency plans if these hurdles are encountered. It should mention triggers that would show risks emerging. It should mention accountability for the risk. These risks and emerging risks should be thought about while doing the risk analysis and while doing month-end reports. Remember to check back with the initial appraisal to ensure that executive's concerns are covered.

Site evaluation is an important piece of the project. Knowing if there is contaminants, infrastructure or soil conditions can have a magnitude of impacts on construction design and construction work. Potential bidders should arrange to see the site before bidding, especially if quoting on a fixed fee basis. Undiscovered site conditions are often the cause of change orders later in the process. Undiscovered site conditions can affect timing, cost and even scope. A hospital in Santa Clara, California, needed to halt construction and get a court order to continue when construction work revealed that the site was an old cemetery.[2]

What is the end goal of this project and how do you expect to get there? This should tie into the investment appraisal and the risk matrix. If the end-all project is to get a Grade A (luxury) office building, you need to use luxury end furniture and flooring. There were times when due to the complexity of the project, the end goal was there, but there were no plans on how to achieve them. During the planning, touchpoints should be put in so any new risks are addressed, and plans can become more tangible. The architect in charge of the Burj Khalifa was solving design problems before they even became problems. This was due to testing that was done during the process. They did wind tunnel testing as the building went up to ensure that the building remained sturdy. This is not a normal procedure but made sense when building the tallest building in the world.

The more detail you can get into while planning, the more you can

- get a better estimate of costs,
- find bidders that will meet your need, and
- establish budgets that are realistic.

PROJECT EXECUTION

Project execution is when most of the activity happens and most of the money is spent. It starts when physical construction starts. This starting point may be different for different projects – it can be demolition, or it can be when the bulldozers start scooping out the foundation. It is not a calendar date – it is solely driven by the activity (even if a calendar date was agreed to).

This requires understanding the deliverables, understanding the budget constraints, and understanding the time constraints. Because the project is most visible at this point, it is important to keep the site presentable yet accessible.

Besides knowing the constraints and the deliverables, the team must work together to monitor and control these two aspects. As mentioned during the pillars of success, the pillars overlap. The team must know the priority of the pillars, as each decision they make impacts these pillars. There is little point in pushing overtime and raising costs to beat a timeline node when the priority is to keep costs down. This phase is complete when the actual construction stops.

Most of the money on the project will be incurred during this phase. Accounting entries should be segregated so you can pinpoint the exact expenses for the project. The accounting entry will look like this:

Construction in Process – 55 Main Street	28000000
Cash	28000000

COMMISSIONING

The commissioning phase occurs when the project is being cleaned up, the labor force is being demobilized and moved to other projects, equipment is returned, and the new owners are trained in whatever they need to know. It is normally not a long phase but does represent a transition. The new owners have a chance to inspect the project and approve it or create a *punch list* of things that still must be completed. A punch list is a list of things that need to be completed to deliver the project in tip-top form. It may include items such as:

- loose wall plates for light switches,
- missing toe guards,
- paint drips,
- paint not finished in corners,
- furnishings, etc.
- Light bulbs needing changing,
- Small alterations.

They are minor items that have little impact on the overall project but still need attention. Usually these are cosmetic items but they don't have to be. At this point any access to the building that the contractor has should be revoked, except for workers doing the punch list items. It is advised that there be some time between this phase and move in so that the punch list items can be completed. Keep in mind that sometimes move in date cannot be moved.

I had one project where they installed AED (defibrillators) on each floor but constructed the worker's desks so close to the AED that in an emergency, you could not reach the AED. The desks were modules and they followed the blueprints. However, the blueprints were done BEFORE the organization decided to install AEDs on every floor. Granted, common sense would be to report this to project management before proceeding. But, alas, it was not done.

OCCUPY AND MOVE IN

During occupancy and move in, the contractors are gone and figuring out final payments. The owners should be tracking, logging and analyzing all issues at move in. This can indicate a problem with one of the vendors or indicate incomplete work.

We did an audit of an apartment building, and it was not until occupancy that an oversight was found. At full occupancy, anyone on the upper floors had no water pressure during 6–8AM (when most residents were getting ready for the day). Though water was tested during the walkthrough, the problem did not manifest itself at that point since there was no large demand for water. Though, this particular finding may be rare, it highlights another problem. Testing of some systems has to wait – i.e. you won't be able to test air conditioning in the middle of winter.

If an employee signs in at their desk and there are no nearby outlets, this would be an issue for the general contractor and possibly the electricians. It is like moving into a new house, you need to be there a few days before you can understand all its' quirks. It is advisable that there is a dedicated hotline in place for occupants to call in with any problems. Data should be compiled and analyzed after move in, one month after, and quarterly after that.

Though move in sounds like a simple process, there are times when move in rehearsals should be done. For example, when moving a hospital to a new location, some items need to be moved quickly such as blood, blood products, certain medications, patients on special equipment, etc. Even moving patients can create a problem, especially patients who cannot really speak for themselves due to age or medical condition. There are also some patients that are in incubators or on life support. How do you move them without harm? I have been involved in several projects like this and what we did was have 'move in fire drills' where the move was practiced, lessons learned were talked about, and details were fixed before the actual move in.

CLOSURE

Closure is the end of the project. Several things happen or should happen during this phase. The one item that is often missed is a lesson learned from the project – what went right, what went wrong? What can be done next time? What did we do correctly? What could we have done better? This is similar to the drills I just talked about. There is no point in having a drill unless you review what could go better.

If internal people were used on the project, you want to do a performance review at the end of the project or be integrated with their annual review. You want to ensure that they can roll back into their previous position, without penalty or prejudice. There should also be an analysis of vendor performance, should the vendor be used again? Why or why not? There should be a way to roll procurement into the fold. We have seen some organizations that use the audit of the project to grade the vendor.

A final reconciliation of the accounts is made, and final retainage is released. Internally, the accounts are closed so that they cannot be used intentionally or erroneously. Lastly, the construction-in-process account is closed and converted to the fixed asset. It is not unusual to wait 3–6 months for this to happen. This is to allow any last-minute bills to come in. However, keeping the accounts open in perpetuity is dangerous.

The entry to close the project account would look something like this:

52 Main Street Property	1290000000	
Construction in Process – 52 Main Street		1290000000

Lessons learned on the project are important but often missed. By systematically conducting lessons-learned sessions and incorporating the insights into future projects, construction teams can improve their efficiency, minimize risks and enhance overall project outcomes. Conducting lessons-learned sessions at the conclusion of a construction project is a valuable practice to identify what went well, what could have been done differently and how to improve processes for future projects. Here's what typically happens during lessons-learned sessions on a construction project:

1. Gather the team together, even players who may not have been on the project for some time, and could include calling audit, as well. I would also invite the executive sponsor. A neutral space should be established and an informal non-accusatory tone be maintained so that people feel safe speaking up.
2. Review the original project plan and look at the goals established early on. Ensure that these goals are met.
3. Celebrate the achievements and recognize quality high points. You want to know what should be replicated in future projects so investigate any special efforts that were made to get to this stage.
4. Specifically ask about obstacles or challenges encountered on the project. Note what had to be done to overcome these challenges.
5. Recognize and document best practices that emerged during the project. These are the strategies, methods or approaches that contributed positively to the project and should be replicated in future endeavors.
6. Evaluate relationships that emerged through the project and list the pros and cons of using these vendors in the future.
7. Review the risk matrix and update it if necessary.
8. Explore any new technology used during the project and discuss whether the technology can be used elsewhere in the organization.
9. Encourage feedback that may not have been asked for and allow team members to have the opportunity to express their opinions.
10. Document what is being said and prepare a report for the project folder.

Lessons learned are a helpful tool. No project is expected to go perfectly but it is prudent to aim for improvement on the next one.

NOTES

1 www.burjkhalifa.ae
2 CBS News Sacramento. May 16, 2012, Crews Building Hospital Halt Construction After Uncovering Lost Cemetery.

Chapter 7

Location and benchmarking

Before you start construction at a site, an important decision has to be made. Where will the project go? This is not as easy as you think. There are so many factors and decisions to be made. One need only look at Brown University in Rhode Island, which used Big Data to do traffic analysis in determining where it would place its $88 million School of Engineering building.[1]

Audit will most likely be joining the project after this decision has been made but they should still look at how the decision was made and signed off on. Were vital errors made or was there no proof or transparency in the decision-making process? Audit should look for any potential conflicts of interest that may have occurred with the acquisition of the property. (We talk about conflict of interest in the next chapter.) Audit's role is to ensure corporate policy is followed. Audit also wants to ensure estimates are current. There have been times when cost estimates are stale and inaccurate.

To understand how the decision was made, audit needs to look at the end goal for the project and evaluate it to ensure the decision made makes sense. For example, if you were to build a mega hotel in Las Vegas, a decision should be made to place in on or near the Strip, rather than 7 miles off the Strip. Based on the goal, some of the decision points that should be considered are as follows:

- Availability to attract target audience (talent for corporate headquarters, tourist attractions for hospitality, easy access for hospitals).
- If people will be accessing your site by car, is parking readily available?
- Is the site close to or near mass transit?
- How attractive is the surrounding area?
- Is the surrounding area 'safe'?
- Would your customer base or employee base need to change conditions to adapt to the new location?
- Is the new location close enough for your existing customer base to continue to come in? Do customers normally come in live?
- Can customers access you via alternate methods (online, telephone, etc.)?
- What kind of visibility would the new site get?

DOI: 10.1201/9781003461487-8

- What are the expected rents or taxes at the site? Are these affordable?
- Is the site going to be carbon neutral?
- Are there nearby hazards (earthquake zone, flooding area, volcano zone, etc.)?
- Are there expected issues with the land as far as usable soil (no contaminants)?
- What was the site previously used for? Will this previous use increase the risk for unknowns? (See the hospital/cemetery example in the previous chapter.)
- Is it legal to have this type of building at the site? (If not, a variance will need to be filed.)

There have been many projects that discover 'surprises' after construction starts. It is important to know what the property was previously used for, so these surprises are not found or are not a 'surprise.' Surprises include unexploded military artifacts, skeletons, historical artifacts, wildlife and contaminants. While building the Burj Khalifa, it was known that the site was a former military base. This had to be considered during construction in the case of finding anything underground.

Keep in mind, audit should not say whether the location picked was a good or bad choice but what it could say is that:

- it aligns with strategic vision.
- it was documented as to why this location was used.
- assumptions made are clearly documented.
- assumptions made were accurate or fairly accurate and timely.
- risks associated with the location were defined and documented.
- currently occurring problems that are due to or close to the site.

An example of a valid exception would be a company that is committed to being carbon neutral, yet, builds a new facility on a plot of land that is predominately forest, deforesting to build the facility and not planting any trees in return.

BENCHMARKING

Many companies will try and shadow projects from one to another. You can see this with many fast-food restaurants, franchises or chain hotels – they all have identical layouts and look exactly alike. Companies who do this may want to benchmark the cost of construction. The problem is, this is possible only if all items are identical. It would be unfair to benchmark a project in Kentucky with a project in midtown Manhattan.

Geographical location is one factor that will throw this off. Luckily, you can get geographical indexes in some of the industry costing guides (Kelly Guides) to better estimate cost and be more accurate in the benchmark. Having a benchmark cost can be helpful if utilizing a design-build contract. We will discuss this in more detail when we talk about contracts. There are, however, other factors that can alter the price of a project – even if benchmarked. These include:

1. Contractor
2. Union Labor Rates
3. Foundation Issues
4. Local variances or building code
5. Price fluctuations in the cost of material
6. Use of surplus materials
7. Reuse of planning documents

The ideal way of benchmarking is not to benchmark just the final costs. Key Performance Indicators (KPIs) need to be identified. These KPIs need to be analyzed to determine if these costs can realistically be met or can be improved. These KPIs don't have to be financial. When benchmarking projects, it makes sense to pull the lessons learned document for the project selected as the comparison project. Delays, for example, are implied costs or lost opportunity costs; improving delays can save money later. Popular KPIs to focus on in construction are:

1. Number of change orders
2. Predictability of costs
3. Cohesiveness of team and team dynamics
4. Profit margins
5. Number of safety concerns
6. Number of items requiring rework
7. Percent of original project budget versus contingency or cumulative change orders.
8. Number of days lost due to third-party interruptions
9. Number of issues upon inspection

Once KPIs are identified, gathering the data is important but sometimes the task seems impossible. The more data you gather with each project (and possibly even with past audits) the easier the task will be. Once the numbers are in and the data has been analyzed it is important to have a collaboration exercise. This involves having all members get together and discuss how things could be changed to improve these KPIs. This goes back to the lessons learned we talked about in the last chapter.

AUDIT STEPS

1. Obtain copies of investment appraisals. Look for any that have benchmarked other projects.
2. Note any assumptions that were adjusted.
3. Understand how adjustments were made.
4. Reconcile adjustments against Kelly guides to determine reasonability.
5. Understand the project objectives and ascertain that comparisons are being made like to like.
6. Define benchmark criteria and identify what standards are being used (industry standards, best practices or internal performance standards).
7. Perform a risk assessment to identify any barriers that may prevent the achievement of project objectives.
8. Assess the adequacy of project planning. Ensure that the objectives and project plans are comparable to the original project.
9. Assess whether the project is allocated adequate resources to be able to mimic performance.
10. Interview stakeholders to assess any concerns or trepidation that they may have.
11. Assess how changes to the project will need to be documented, priced and approved prior to work being done.
12. Promote compatibility but improvement.

NOTE

1 We Build Value – Big Data in Construction Projects, Digital Magazine, May 15, 2018.

Chapter 8

Conflicts of interest

A conflict of interest occurs when an entity or individual becomes unreliable because of a clash between personal (or self-serving) interests and professional duties or responsibilities. Such a conflict occurs when a company or person has a vested interest – such as money, status, knowledge, relationships or reputation – which puts into question whether their actions, judgment or decision-making can be unbiased. In the case of construction, this can be that a person has a stake in the property being acquired or they have arrangements or interests with vendors that will be working on the project. When the goals of the person do not coincide with the goals of the project, difficulties follow. The goals of the project are to get high quality with the least cost (usually).

Here are some steps on how to investigate a potential conflict-of-interest on a construction project:

1. Ensure that everyone on the project – executive sponsor, facility manager, procurement director, project manager, etc. has signed a conflict-of-interest statement with personnel or with the contract.
2. Identify the potential conflict of interest. This could involve identifying any relationships between the parties involved in the project that could give rise to a conflict of interest.

   For example, if a contractor is related to a project manager, this could create a conflict of interest if the contractor is awarded the contract. The easiest way to determine if there is a conflict of interest is to have, market and encourage the use of a fraud hotline.

   It is harder to audit for a conflict of interest (though not impossible) than it is to have a hint as to where to start. It is also suggested that you audit for a conflict of interest by receiving payroll data and cash disbursement journals of the general contractor and looking for the names of executives, procurement personnel, and children or spouses of each of these.

   Potential red flags include close personal relationships, undisclosed relationships, unusual bidding patterns, sole-sourced bidders, bidders

DOI: 10.1201/9781003461487-9

with an unusually fast response time, generous gifts and hospitality and vendors that continue to get repeat work despite poor performance.

Look at social media to see if people appear closer on social media than in a normal business relationship.

3. Gather evidence. Once you have identified a potential conflict, you will need to gather evidence to support your claim. This could include documents, e-mails, or other records that show the existence of the conflict of interest. Before checking e-mails, consult with an IT audit so that you can read them without impeding evidence rules or confidentiality. If you can find that the parties acknowledged the conflict of interest, all the better. Scouting their social media accounts can reveal intent or knowledge. Interviews and interrogations will need to be done.

   On a specific audit, there were allegations that the facility manager was paying too many favors to the external project manager. The facility manager claimed that they had just met for this project. A review of social media showed a recent celebration, the christening of project manager's daughter. The Godfather was the facility manager. It was enough evidence to show both and they admitted that they had known each other for a long time, well before the project started.
4. Interview the parties involved. It is important to interview the parties involved in the project to get their perspective on the potential conflict of interest. This will help you to understand the facts of the case and to determine whether there is a genuine conflict of interest. It is possible there is a conflict but that it was innocent or within policy. For example, I found a conflict once and during the interview the employee (a purchasing agent) admitted that one company belonged to her uncle. Her uncle bid on the project and when she noticed she recused herself from the selection. She had documented it with an e-mail to her superior and to the head of the construction project. She did not reveal the name of the company so as not to unduly persuade the rest of the team to vote for her. An audit revealed no irregularities or indications that the winning vendor received favors to be selected.
5. Make a decision. Once you have gathered all the evidence and interviewed the parties involved, you will need to decide whether there is a conflict of interest. If you believe that there is a conflict of interest, you will need to take steps to address it.
6. Be objective and fair. It is important to be objective and fair when investigating a potential conflict of interest. You should not let your own personal biases or opinions influence your decision.
7. Follow the rules. There may be specific rules or regulations that govern conflicts of interest in the construction industry or in the jurisdiction. Speak to Legal. You should make sure that you are familiar with these rules and that you follow them when investigating a potential conflict of interest. There may be internal policies in effect – such as signing of conflict-of-interest policies or ethics clauses (see Step 1).

8. Keep records. It is important to keep records of your investigation. This will help you to document your findings and to defend your decision if it is challenged. It is particularly important if the person with the conflict of interest will possibly be terminated.

It is best to know some ways that conflicts of interest appear in a project. A bribe is usually defined as the giving or receiving of a 'thing of value' to corruptly influence the actions of another, most commonly to influence a contract award or the execution of a contract. A 'kickback' is a bribe paid by the contractor after it is paid. Most bribes in exchange for large contract awards in international development projects are paid as kickbacks, usually 5%–20% of the contract value. The bribe does not need to be money and many are not.

1. Site visits – An executive or procurement person is invited to visit the site where the goods are being made or where the marble is being quarried. This sounds innocent enough; it becomes a problem when the other party pays for it. They normally pay for first-class flights and deluxe accommodations. Travel plans for the project should be paid by the owner and we will talk more about this with layering fraud.
2. Large donations – Donations can be used as a conflict of interest when they affect the decision-making or actions of a person or an organization in a way that is not in the best interest of their mission or beneficiaries. For example, if a charity trustee accepts a donation from a donor who expects them to use it for a specific purpose that is not aligned with the charity's goals. If a non-profit employee receives a personal benefit from a donor who wants to influence their work, these are conflicts of interest.

   Beware of donations you may not be able to see, such as donations to a charity that an executive or procurement person has a vested stake in outside the organization. We found one incidence where the contractor received favorites due to being a major sponsor at a charity golf tournament that the client held annually.
3. Employment and internships – A conflict of interest can occur if one party hires an employee or family matter in return for favors on the project such as being the chosen vendor or influencing the project leader on the project to 'look the other way.' Another method that has been seen, they promise the children of the conflicted person employment or internships.
4. Standard kickbacks – Some may think it is easy to just look at a cash disbursement journal to find kickbacks. Alas, many times the vendors are a lot more creative. One of the common ways to hide this from the cash disbursements register is to 'accidentally' overbill and then issue a refund. The problem is the refund goes back to an individual, not to the owner organization.

5. Loans – Loans may come in the form of advancing money for the project or offering to help secure project funding. They often do not require any paying back of the loan.
6. Overpayments and overbills – As a way to legitimize and to allow a bribe to be deductible, the company will purposely overbill for an invoice, equipment or other item. It gets paid via normal routes in the organization. At that point the briber refunds the overpayment back to the organization. The refund check is made out to a person and instead of the organization getting the money back, the employee gets it.
7. Unqualified testing or vetting before bidding – A member of procurement will allow a vendor to bid and be selected even though they have not been vetted or they may have failed the vetting process. This one, ideally, should be easy to prove. The procurement file should be missing the vetting process or based on records spent, auditor should see that they did not meet the vendor qualifications.
8. Overstock – Company will purposely buy access material or equipment and offers a return for excess material. A refund is made, similar to overpayments and overbills. In some cases, the material will be material the conflicted person wants. Look for delivery addresses other than the project. Look for material delivered to the site that never makes it into site inventory. Look for material in a small quantity that does not match what is being used on the project.

Red flags are:

- Unexplained or unusual favoritism of a particular contractor or vendor
- Contracting or purchasing employee lives beyond means
- Employee has discussions about employment with a current or prospective vendor
- Close socialization with and acceptance of inappropriate gifts, travel or entertainment from a vendor
- Procurement employee appears to conduct side business

CASE STUDY

There is a procurement official, Kelly. Kelly oversees sourcing vendors for a capital construction project. She was working for a corporate office while obtaining her degree in fashion design. While going to school she met an individual, Tom, who was going to the same school to become a history major. Tom had a small company working as a project manager. The company was not doing well as all the 'bigger' firms kept winning the bids. They worked in New York City, and he felt that he could earn more as a project manager by working on historical buildings.

Her corporate headquarters were located just off of 5th Avenue in Manhattan (aka Fashion Row). Her goal was to open her own clothing boutique of evening gowns. To fund and furnish the clothing line she was building up her stock now. She had a completed series of dresses already made and had plans in place for another line. She had secured a set of workers to sew the dresses for her next collection.

One night after class, Tom and Kelly grabbed a coffee. She told him about the capital construction project her organization was doing. She casually mentioned that the building was protected and there were certain actions that would have to be taken to preserve the façade. Tom was intrigued. He told her he would love to get involved with that project and if she could help him, he knew of an empty storefront for her fashion line. He knew that he would not pass the background check as he had only been in business a few months. He even offered the services of his company to help her turn the storefront into a great boutique.

Kelly agreed to get him on the vendor list. Besides, she knew with him being a new business, Tom would put in a low bid. And so he did. In fact, it was so low Kelly told him to resubmit at a higher cost and she promised him he would be selected. Tom won the job and was in charge of project management and furnishing the new building. Tom and Kelly worked closely together on the project and built up a close friendship. Kelly was soon to graduate and was desperate to get the store running. She was getting so excited it was all she could talk about to Tom. But she was worried. It would take so long for her to get the funds together to order the last of what they needed for the store.

Kelly and Tom came up with a plan. Since Tom was shopping for furnishings for the projects, he could order 'extra' for Kelly. He approved the invoices, no one would notice. Kelly and Tom proceeded and were able to open Kelly's store. Kelly was preparing to leave the project but wanted to see the project out and accrue just a bit more money. Besides, they felt that if Kelly left now, the new person taking over may uncover what she and Tom were doing.

Audit came along and noted that 5000 hangers were ordered for the new building. It was put in on 12 different change orders. Kelly claimed the change orders were split up so that the hangers would be delivered to specific locations. Audit questioned the quantity and Kelly explained this was to accommodate guests. Each cubicle got 1 hangar and certain individuals got more for guests. There were 385 offices.

Further investigation revealed that the hangers went to Kelly's new store. Further audit revealed more additional furnishings, including LCD TV screens, curtains, cash registers, and a couch. Audit did not initially question the cash registers as there would be a cafeteria and two coffee stands in the building.

Kelly and Tom were ordered to pay restitution and were both terminated.

Chapter 9

Project appraisal

The first step in doing a construction or capital improvement project is determining that a project is needed. It should be an answer to another business issue, and this is important as it sets a goal for the project. It is important that an auditor applies a great deal of common sense when accepting that this was a good project to do. A project presented to the committee can be denied, accepted or conditionally accepted – accepted with constraints or modification. The auditor cannot say whether it was the correct answer, but they can confirm that it is done in compliance with policies and procedures around capital improvements and is in line with strategic operations of the company.

An auditor can attest to the fact that the approval or decision process was transparent and documented as such. They can also point out any control issues or errors with the investment decision. This step is called Project Conception, as it represents when an idea is first conceived.

In an ideal world, the investment decision will be submitted to a corporate committee for review. (This is known as business case analysis.) There should be

- a goal,
- a description of the problem (or reason for the project),
- a description of the project,
- the person who will sponsor the project (preferably, another executive). There may be no sponsor assigned at this phase, some organizations assign the sponsor on project acceptance,
- and an estimate of costs. In many cases, the cost is a one-line number. Submitting costs as a one-line figure is a weakness and procedures should state, or be amended, to show costs broken down by line item. This will make more sense later.

There should be enough information about the project so that executives can compare it against other solutions to the problem. Any assumptions should be listed in the case, and assumptions about cost or final outcome should be clearly explained. The auditor should review this and verify that

DOI: 10.1201/9781003461487-10

these assumptions are reasonable. Preferably they will have documented evidence that supports the assumptions. This is just one of the reasons why the costs should be broken down by line items. Documented evidence can include labor reports, estimates prepared by an independent party, screen-shots of market costs, or market valuation reports. An auditor, feeling that the numbers are inaccurate, may seek expertise from an expert. This is an acceptable practice but should be disclosed in the audit report:

- Who was hired?
- Why was this party selected?
- What was the scope of their assignment?
- What was the result they came up with?
- How much did the service cost?

The auditor should obtain a copy of the business case when starting their audit. Occasionally there may be notes on the case where the committee requires certain things (color scheme, budget, time frame, safety concerns, lessons learned from past projects) these should be noted and tested by the auditor.

As I am writing this guide, the world is returning to normal after suffering from a pandemic, a black swan event (an event that was unexpected but has far-reaching and disastrous consequences). When a black swan occurs, it is likely that the costs and assumptions made in the business case are stale and should be updated to reflect current market conditions. Additionally, projects may no longer be needed. Projects approved but not started should have to go through the approval process again.

Keep in mind that the projects being considered may or may not all be construction. It can be Information Technology, Human Resource Initiatives, merger, acquisition, new product line, etc. They should align with the long-term strategic goals of the organization.

Once the investment committee approves the project it will move to the project initiation phase. It will answer two questions:

1. Is the project feasible (and at what cost)?
2. Is the project of value?

Value is the value that the project will create for end users. It may be subjective rather than an actual dollar amount. Examples would include increased efficiency for the department, the ability to handle more customers over a longer period of time, compliance with rules and regulations of governing bodies, etc. Value should be compared to cost – what is it going to cost to undertake the project? Sometimes (especially if the project is to satisfy regulatory or compliance requirements) the cost may be larger than the value, but it must be done anyway. This should be documented in the business case analysis.

RED FLAG FOR ISSUES WITH BUSINESS CASE ANALYSIS

1. Talking to executives, they complain that they put projects in, but they never get approved.
2. One executive constantly getting all his projects approved.
3. Fraud Hotline Tip. Do not underestimate the tips that come in, they can be of great value in identifying problems.
4. Disrepair around the corporate campus when more funding is going for new infrastructure.
5. Computers that keep crashing (include networks and printers) and yet all IT projects are getting canceled.
6. Vendors that get reused from one project to another – especially if the vendor did not do a quality job.
7. A known project with failures is used as a foundation (benchmark) for other projects.

The policies and procedures around business case analysis should already exist in the organization. The business case decisions are usually a quarterly occurrence and if the auditor wants to observe one, it may be possible. They will need approval from the executive committee to observe. As stated earlier, the business case analysis should be obtained before starting the construction audit. Here we will discuss how the decision is made and highlight key controls in the process. If they are not granted permission to be at the meeting, there should still be minutes of the meeting that will highlight the approval process.

The Business Case Analysis should start with the introduction of a project in a summary for the executives. It should answer

- **why** the project is being considered or why it should be the answer to a problem,
- **how** the concept came to be,
- **who** supports this and who will be affected (we will discuss key stakeholders later),
- **what** the project will entail and
- **when** it could be started, as well as the proposed schedule of events,
- Finally, it should include what the cost of undertaking the project will be.

Having detailed figures will help you compare the planned to the actual later. In case of cost overruns, you will need that as a starting point for an audit.

Chapter 10

Investment decision-making

The executive committee has a few decisions to make. They need to answer the big question of how much is available for investment and what project(s) will be invested in. It is not so easy as reading the business case analysis and picking one. It is normally more methodical and systematic.

The executive committee will be looking for a *return on investment (ROI)*, An ROI answers the question: *what do we receive for what we spend?* This is usually expressed as a ratio. A positive ROI means that the project will return more than the cost of the project. There will ideally be a profit for undertaking this initiative. Though rare, it is possible to have an ROI of 0 – this means there is no loss or benefit for the cost. A negative ROI means that the cost of the project far outweighs the value. This results in a net loss. Sometimes a project has to be done, despite the ROI. When multiple projects are proposed the project with the highest ROI should be the one selected (Table 10.1). If denied, there should be a written reason on either the proposal itself or recorded as minutes to the selection meeting.

$$\text{Simple ROI} = \frac{(\text{Gains} - \text{Investment Costs})}{\text{Investment Costs}}$$

Keep in mind that the cost and benefit are 'guesstimates' they are not actual figures. They are at most predictions on the cost and benefit. It may

Table 10.1 Project evaluation simple ROI

Project number	*Cost*	*Benefit*	*ROI*	*Interpretation*
1	£100,000	£150,000	50%	Favorable outcome and should be project selected
2	£100,000	£110,000	10%	Favorable outcome
3	£100,000	£100,000	0	Neutral outcome
4	£110,000	£100,000	−10%	Net loss, unfavorable outcome

DOI: 10.1201/9781003461487-11

or may not include indirect costs. Normally, the cost of any related audits is not included.

Be careful when looking at a business case analysis that uses just ROI. ROI does not take into effect all risk factors. So, while ROI can be used to select one project over another, it should not be used as the **only** factor. It makes the assumption that costs are as they are 'hoped for.'

I was once asked to evaluate a project case analysis for a renovation of an apartment building. It assumed that the current full occupancy would continue, despite rental increases. Rental increases went from below market rates to market rates. This doubled the rent on some apartments and tripled on some. At below-market rates there were waiting lists for apartments. After the project was done the new rates went into effect. Occupancy dropped over 40% and there was a net loss recognized. Many apartments remained vacant.

The use of ROI can be very helpful when answering the following:

- Should we make this investment?
- Will the investment be a gain or a loss?
- How profitable can this project be?
- Which option is the most profitable?

Again, the benefits and the costs are only assumptions of the person proposing the project. Sometimes you will see ROI being used in situations where it should not be used. These should be noted as audit exceptions.

- Do not use ROI when cash inflow and cash outflow are not available.
- Be careful if returns are not probably defined. If a project entails new construction and it will provide revenue of £2 million, the inflow is not $2 million, it is the difference between the £2 million minus the inflows for doing nothing.
- ROI should not be used for investments covering different periods. Returns on project A may show inflow over the next four years. Returns on project B may show inflow over the next seven years. They can not be compared to each other. Other things need to be equal to make a fair comparison.
- Do not use ROI if you cannot isolate the inflow or outflow figures that are solely due to each project.

Assume that you are building a radiology lab for a hospital. This will put an extra burden on registrars. If the registrar must be there for non-radiology services, how is the cost of the radiology services alone isolated? If the investment is for marketing services, can outflows be truly appropriated to the marketing services? Other factors such as customer service and overall reputation of the organization need to be considered.

In some instances, you will see that ROI is calculated based on discounted cash flow. With a discounted cash flow, income figures and outcome figures are 'normalized' to come up with present values. This can make a lot of sense with construction projects as construction generally spans several years. You may be able to increase revenue by £2 million a year but when does the revenue-earning potential actually start?

An auditor looking at this should ensure that the same method of normalizing the figures on the projects is done. They should be normalized on the same basis over the same period of time. Interpreting what the present value is can invoke serious challenges. Many businesspeople struggle with this. Because of that, it is rarely seen. However, there are ways to program spreadsheets to calculate net present value (NPV) for you. Complicating this further, a project that has more costs at the beginning of the project (also known as Front-loaded) will normally result in a reduced ROI than if the case was not discounted.

NPV is another way to compare projects to determine in which to invest. NPV is one way of placing multiple alternatives or solutions into a common frame of reference. It factors in the future value of an income stream based on a discounted rate. The best place to validate the discount rate is with the Treasury Management department. It is based on expectations of inflation or the expected return on money invested. The premise comes into play by assuming that money earned in the future is not as valuable as the same amount of money if received today. The rate should be based on some sort of validation – it may be an ROI that the company has historically seen. It considers the opportunity cost or cost loss by not putting the money into a typical investment scheme.

Inflation is the process in which the dollar value of money rises over time. If you had the money presently, you could spend it presently. If you do not get the money until five years from now, you cannot spend it for five years. If the money is not spent today it could expect to fall over time based on an implied annual rate. This implied rate is the rate used to discount the cash and normalize it. There is no guarantee that the rate used is correct, the rate is highly subjective. The auditor should get an understanding of how treasury management derived the rate used.

In comparison, future value is the value of an asset in the future based on an assumed rate of growth. It considers that business grows at an assumed rate. It generally results in a more accurate picture of what each investment project offers. Both present value and future value are prone to criticism, as no interest rate or return is guaranteed. Swings in inflation can erode the calculated rate of return on an investment.

Expected costs, if not estimated accurately, will alter the profitability. This sometimes will come down to accepting a project by one executive director over another, because that executive has more success in project management. If this is the case, it should be documented in the business case.

To calculate the value by using either a future rate or a discounted rate, three things must be determined:

1. Expected cash flows (both in and out)
2. The number of years the cash flow is expected to be spread over
3. The discount rate

The importance of present value is to make sure when comparing different scenarios, you can get a true picture across different scenarios and still create a common core or level.

Though I have often seen NPV used in making investment decisions, we often see Internal Rate of Return (IRR) IRR is the same as NPV but the rate for discounting cash is the ACTUAL return that the organization has experienced. This rate should be calculated and provided by Treasury Management as there are many components or factors used when calculating the IRR. Audit should determine how Treasury Management calculated IRR.

The Payback Period is what I call the Wimpy Model. In the 1930s, Wimpy was a cartoon character in the comic strip Popeye. Wimpy would 'Gladly pay you Tuesday for a hamburger today.' The payback period for Wimpy is the number of days until Tuesday. (In actuality, Wimpy stayed home on Tuesday so as not to have to pay for advanced burgers). In business it is the amount of time until you see a return on your investment. Going back to the radiology example, how long it will take to get 'paid back' is rather simple to calculate if you can map out costs and returns. The payback period is how long it will take until you break even on the project. If you invest £2 million for a five-year project and you can make £400,000 a year in Radiology services it will take you ten years to get paid back (five years for construction plus five years' worth of revenue). The project with the smallest payback period is the one that should be selected.

The payback period does not take into effect the time value of money. The payback period is simple to calculate and is often used for that reason. It is argued that the project with the smallest payback period is symbolic of the level of liquidity of a project. Use of the payback period ignores the value an organization will eventually make on salvage or scrap value.

Another method we see is a SWOT analysis. This is generally used when looking at retail operations that are deciding where to build further branches. SWOT stands for:

Strength – subjectively, what internal advantages does an organization have that make the project seem profitable? If they have a lot of customers in one state and little offices, a new office will take advantage of the strength of the market base.

Weakness – subjectively, what does the organization lack that would put the project at great risk of failing? If the organization would open in a state does the organization have the organizational assets to operate there?

Opportunities – subjectively, what is the benefit of overtaking a project? Are locals looking for a business like the one provided by the organization? Is there a need in the location for an organization such as this?

Threats – subjectively, what exterior forces exist that put the project at risk? If you are opening a coffee shop, are there too many competitors nearby? Is the marketplace already saturated? Have other companies failed there? Why?

Regardless of the method used the importance from an audit standing is that all projects are evaluated on the same basis and the basis is appropriate for the problem addressed. There should be room in procedures to use an alternate method of evaluating projects if appropriate. Specifically, projects being done to meet regulatory guidelines may need to take precedence over more desirable projects, regardless of the investment and return. As an example, companies that wanted to reopen after the pandemic needed to invest in signage, hand washing facilities, and other measures to prevent the spread of the disease and meet minimum requirements to open. This project (if it is important to reopen offices) may take precedence over something like building a new radiology suite or upgrading IT systems.

Once the project is approved, the executive committee should document that they approve the project, how much they are committing to the project, and should document what their expectations are. It should include a brief sentence of project goals and a charter about the project. If an executive sponsor will be used, the sponsor should be named on the documentation.

Procedures should be written that state what the requirements are around project documentation. Additionally, there should be a templated form for them to file – this will ensure that all information is registered.

Chapter 11

ESG and construction

ESG stands for Environmental, Social and Governance. It is a set of criteria that investors, businesses and other stakeholders use to assess and measure the sustainability and ethical impact of a company or organization. ESG is not just about your investment portfolio as some think. It is in your actions, your words, your plans and yes, in your construction.

Here's a brief overview of each component:

1. **Environmental (E)**: This aspect focuses on a company's impact on the environment. It includes considerations such as the company's carbon footprint, energy efficiency, waste management practices, water usage and commitment to renewable energy sources. Companies with strong environmental practices aim to minimize their negative impact on the environment and promote sustainable practices. In construction, this can commonly encompass what materials go into the end design. For example, concrete is environmentally unfriendly so some projects are using hemp bound with a lime to replace concrete. Using sustainably sourced bamboo for flooring would be another idea. Auditors may lack the expertise to determine if a project is environmentally friendly. In lieu of the expertise, interview the architect and ask how the environment was considered.

   Just like value engineering looks for value during the design phase, the same can be done with ESG. As the architect plans and designs the project, they should be looking for switching out materials for more environmentally friendly materials. Sometimes it can also come down to where the material is sourced. Some vendors will use biodegradable packaging and some vendors will use more socially acceptable delivery methods. (Overnight deliveries can sometimes be more environmentally friendly.)
2. **Social (S)**: The social dimension of ESG relates to how a company manages its relationships with employees, customers, suppliers, communities and other stakeholders. Key areas include employee welfare, diversity and inclusion, human rights, labor practices, product safety, customer satisfaction and community engagement.

DOI: 10.1201/9781003461487-12

Socially responsible companies strive to be fair, transparent and accountable to all stakeholders. Controls in place around identifying and protecting trafficking victim would be an example. In construction there have been trends of contractors using traffic victims or illegal immigrants and paying them 'under the table' so they can pay a lower wage and not pay tax. On paper they pay legitimate or fictitious employees.

It is important that an auditor audit the payroll and look for missing social security numbers, illogical patterns of social security numbers (consecutive numbers), or if possible, social security numbers tied to people too old or too young to be working on the site. This is a good test to do through data analytics if you can get electronic copies of payroll.

The second aspect of social initiative has to do with more and more females entering the construction arena. Efforts have to be made to ensure she has conditions similar to all the men, locker or changing rooms that are separated from the men, and possibly even separate Porta Potty facilities. Procedures or rules may need to be implemented into conditions of locker rooms, images displayed in locker rooms and other shared facilities.

Construction legislation will soon require that supplying personally protective equipment (PPE) is not enough. The new requirements will require that PPE must be properly fitting equipment. This would require that they stock spare PPE in special sizes to meet individual needs. It may also mean that women on-site may need special notification or reimbursement for safety equipment. Construction boots, especially steel-toed, are often only available in larger men's sizes. This may require advance notice to order from online sources to get the needed equipment.

3. **Governance (G)**: Governance refers to the framework of rules, systems and processes that guide a company's decision-making and control mechanisms. Good governance ensures that a company operates ethically, transparently and with accountability. Areas of focus include
   - board composition,
   - executive compensation,
   - shareholder rights,
   - anti-corruption policies, and
   - adherence to legal and regulatory standards.

   ESG criteria are often used by investors to assess the sustainability and ethical performance of companies they consider for investment. These criteria help investors identify companies that are managing environmental and social risks effectively and that have strong corporate governance practices in place. Additionally, ESG considerations can also influence consumer choices and impact a company's reputation in the marketplace. As sustainability and ethical concerns gain prominence in the business world, ESG has become an essential framework for evaluating a company's overall impact on society and the environment.

Construction depletes raw materials. The material used will be the responsibility of the architect. But organizations can be more ESG compliant by specifying how and where they will source the material. Vendors may be evaluated on how they comply with ESG in their operations:

- How does the company enhance their environmental impact?
- How does a vendor harvest raw materials? How do they adapt, reuse and recycle materials?
- Can a vendor provide or validate the environmental impact of their projects? Other factors can be used to evaluate how the construction project is operating and may come down to small details around canteen areas, water stations and safety standards. Ethical labor practices around working conditions and even overtime will make an impact on the carbon footprint of the project. The choice of equipment or particulate filters on equipment can be other ways to generate more responsibility toward environmental issues.

Sourcing of labor impacts ESG under the social component. Companies may need to prove the sustainability of their labor force. How are the companies being used investing in their labor force: health, safety, well-being, sick pay and staff development are all areas that should be noted.

The impact of construction activities on neighbors and passersby should also be considered. Construction projects create pollution – particulates in the air, noise pollution and possibly light pollution. All these factors impact those close to the site. Some ways to mitigate this include barricades and perimeter fencing around the construction, adherence to curfews and exercising care when planning loud activities – such as demolition and controlled explosions. Additionally, having open communication with residents will also help.

Many companies, when choosing to invest, invest in those organizations that have a strong ESG profile. This means the ramifications of ESG on the project extend a lot further and wider than just the project being done.

Projects need to upskill employees and train them on ESG solutions that they can implement. There are suites of solutions out there and the labor force needs to know how to access them and understand how they can deliver carbon reductions.

Once contractors spread the knowledge and accountability to the labor force, it is important to tackle supply issues and subcontractor issues. This is a challenge as it falls somewhere out of their sphere of control. They should choose to work with companies that have a strong ESG profile or who have creative solutions in place to reduce their carbon footprint. Fostering positive vendor relationships can help strengthen ESG impact as companies can work with their subcontractors and suppliers to focus on better practices – low-traffic delivery schedules, shipping more frequently in smaller vehicles, reducing the use of plastic in supply deliveries, etc.

ESG is more than just a buzzword. It is here to stay and failing to consider ESG is a gift we are taking away from future generations. It is not just about sound business practices, sound investment options and corporate responsibility. It is about accepting responsibility and empowering our people and practices to do the same.

Chapter 12

Building the construction team

Vendors will need to be selected. This is where Audit will normally start the review. I recommend going all the way back to the decision-making process. Failure to do so may mean that important issues are ignored.

Building the team is the goal and job of the procurement team. Before you just pass by this chapter, keep in mind that the procurement function is different with construction projects than it is with normal organizational procurement. First off, as I mentioned in the previous chapter, recommendations for vendor selection and who to send bids to may be left up to the general contractor. Owners must be diligent to protect their interests and their voices at the bidding table. If they don't, they are relinquishing too much control. Much of the bidding and opening of bids may be done off-site and may be led by the project manager or the architect. At the end of the day, the owner pays for the work and should be present at the bid opening and should have a proportionate share (or higher) of the vote over the winning vendor.

But picking the correct vendor is tricky. Criteria must be established for the project that answers – what is important in this project. That answer can vary. For example, criteria may be around reputation, history for safety, experience in this type of construction, past experience, ESG profile, and for some, cost. Price is important, but it may not be the biggest determination. Before the project goes out to bid, the procurement team should choose and document the criteria by which bids will be judged. Careful, when selecting the bidders, you want to ensure that the selection complies with your company's ESG and MWBE initiatives.

Be careful when vetting experience. Residential construction is not the same as infrastructure construction. Commercial construction is not the same as residential construction. It is prudent to vet the vendor by looking at their portfolio to see what type of work they have done in the past.

The project is assigned a project team, project charter and possibly project manager. The auditor should determine who is on the team and who is in charge. Be careful when being told who the project manager is. It can be someone internal to the organization or it can be an external vendor to the organization. In some cases, it is both. This can be quite confusing, but I will

DOI: 10.1201/9781003461487-13

reiterate below the different roles. The earlier audit can get their arms around this, the easier the audit will be.

Internal Project Manager – An internal project manager is one who makes the decisions and protects the interest of the organization to ensure construction is done to plan, vendors are procured and managed, budgets are updated and communicated to management, and they act as the liaison between the construction team and the organization's management. Typical duties include:

- Identify key stakeholders and learn what stakeholders' expectations are; manage to these expectations.
- Develop detailed project plans and work schedules; revise as necessary,
- Monitor and report on project performance.
- Identify project tasks and assign them out to the team as deemed appropriate to skill set and experience.
- Report project status and progress to upper management.
- Develop leadership to the project team, project customers, and other project stakeholders.
- Build and manage vendor relationships.

If an internal project manager is being used, they are normally an employee of the organization. There is no need to go through procurement, they will be assigned to the work, but you will need to select one that has the requisite experience and availability to oversee the project. Many internal project managers may specialize in project management and IT work. Construction is a different skill set than IT so the selector should consider this in their choice.

In the above definition we mention key stakeholders. Key stakeholders are those individuals or organizations that have a significant interest in the project, its outcomes, and its processes. They can be internal or external to the organization and can have various levels of impact or pressure (or none at all) on the project.

Key stakeholders are considered crucial to the success of the project and a good project team will know what the stakeholders want or expect. Engaging and managing their expectations can be vital to the project. Note, however, that I say their expectations must be managed not necessarily met. There are stakeholders who will want or need information, who will ask for certain things and not get it, or who will think they possess more power over a project than they actually do. Managing expectations is about understanding who key stakeholders are, prioritizing their expectations, and allocating resources to those that you can – within reason. For example, I had an executive who wanted a mahogany desk and a private bathroom for his new office. However, company policy identified the type of furnishings that each level was entitled to. He was not entitled to a private bathroom or mahogany furnishings. In this project we had to carefully let him know we could not meet that expectation and why.

Key stakeholders can be broken down as follows Figure 12.1:

1. Regulators and government agencies – Authorities that oversee the project and ensure compliance with relevant rules and regulations. The most common example of this is the zoning boards and building code enforcers. Enforcers will inspect the property and issue certificates of use or occupancy. Without this the organization may not be able to 'use' the project. In some instances, you will need several enforcers like building code officers, fire inspectors and elevator inspectors.
2. Suppliers and vendors – Those parties that will sell or rent material or equipment for the project and those who will provide labor for the services needed for the project.
3. Employees and workers – Those within the organization that will be directly or indirectly impacted by the project.
4. Community and interest groups – External groups or committees affected by the project's outcomes. Neighbors would fall into this group.

An external project manager is a company or individual hired to act as a liaison between the owner organization and all members/vendors of the construction team. Sometimes there will be an argument that says, 'I have a project manager, so we don't have to do an audit'. Unfortunately, that is incorrect and if perpetrated can be very costly to the organization. I am not saying it is bad to use one, but it does not replace the need for an audit. Several reasons:

- They are generally paid as a percentage of the invoices for the month, this is an impediment to independence.
- Audit will look at the work of the project manager as well as the overall construction project.
- Audit can confirm adherence to internal policies and procedures.
- Many of the vendors were recommended or selected by the project manager and therefore, independence is again, compromised.

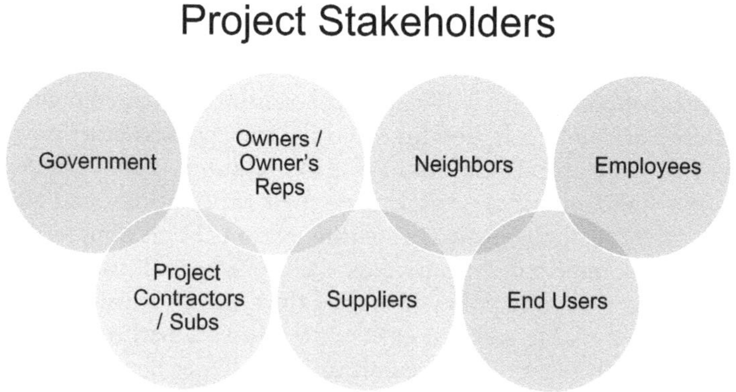

Figure 12.1 Potential project stakeholders.

Audit should be used for both routine inquiries and procedures built into the construction process as well as a vehicle to handle executive concerns.

There may be criteria around using local or MWBE vendors. This may be that you must use minority or women-owned businesses on the project. If you require this, be cautioned, MWBE fraud is prevalent. In MWBE fraud, the vendor who is hired uses the logo of an MWBE firm and places the same on one of their trucks, vans, or other equipment. This is generally easy to do. To do this you would need to obtain a magnetic logo of the MWBE. You can generally order these online and they cost around $25–40 each. There is no large cash investment to perpetrate this fraud. In March 2023, Manhattan prosecutors indicted eight companies and six companies, operating as JM3 Construction Enterprises, for multimillion-dollar MWBE fraud. In this case, JM3 used the MWBEs to bid on projects and then JM3 did the worker using illegal workers and minors. If they got hurt, which they did, they were coached to lie to medical professionals as to how the injury came about.[1]

Ensure that the owner verifies that the MWBE is on premises to do work. Additionally, it may be worth calling the MWBE firm to ensure they plan on working on the project. Review the sign-in logs or payroll reports to ensure employees of the MWBE appear on-site.

SAMPLE MWBE AUDIT

- Conduct comprehensive due diligence on potential MWBE partners before entering into any agreements.
- Verify that Bidding Document referred to MWBE participation.
- Verify the legitimacy of the MWBE's ownership, qualifications and certifications. Note if pre-qualification of MWBE status was done.
- Establish clear policies and procedures for engaging MWBEs, including procurement processes and vendor selection criteria.
- Ensure that these policies are communicated to all relevant stakeholders within the organization and on the construction team.
- Implement regular internal audits to assess the effectiveness of MWBE programs and to detect any irregularities.
- Monitor MWBE performance and financial transactions to identify any suspicious activities (imposters).
- Maintain thorough documentation of the MWBE selection process, contract agreements and performance evaluations.
- Seek external validation of certifications and ownership.
- Establish confidential whistleblower programs to encourage employees and stakeholders to report any suspicions of fraud or non-compliance.
- Ensure protection for individuals who report concerns in good faith.
- Clearly outline expectations and deliverables in contracts with MWBEs.

- Implement oversight mechanisms to ensure that MWBEs fulfill their contractual obligations.
- Conduct random audits and on-site visits to MWBEs to verify that they are operating in accordance with the terms of the contract and applicable regulations.
- Conduct random audits and on-site visits and ask workers for government-issued IDs; confirm identity and vouch back to payroll records.
- Verify their presence on-site during on-site visits. Be careful of vehicles labeled with the name of the company, these are often fictitious.
- Implement technology solutions, such as data analytics and monitoring tools, to identify patterns or anomalies in financial transactions related to MWBEs.
- Work collaboratively with relevant regulatory agencies to stay informed about any changes in MWBE regulations and to seek guidance on compliance.
- Regularly review and update anti-fraud measures to adapt to changing risks and regulations.
- Learn from any instances of fraud or non-compliance to strengthen future prevention efforts.

What else might you want to know about a vendor before choosing them for the project? How about:

- How many years of relevant experience can they demonstrate?
- How many years of existence (be careful, some new firms are old firms with new names or small changes in management) do they possess?
- Can they provide proof of financial stability via an independent source?
- Can they adequately staff and schedule the project with workers who have the requisite expertise?
- Have employees been certified as to safety handling licenses via OSHA or another regulator?
- Are they an incumbent vendor or a vendor used before?
- What has the organization done as far as ESG initiative?
- What is their MWBE status?
- Are they a union shop or non-union?
- Ability to get insurance.
- History of violations
- Relevant experience in this TYPE of construction, different types have different skill sets needed, (i.e. medical, nuclear, etc.)
- Highly recommended or referred.

There are several ways to get the information and answers to above.

1. Check their website. This helps you determine whether the company is legitimate and is the company that is advertised.
2. Run background reports, careful though some background reports (such as Dunn and Bradstreet and Hoovers) are self-reported and the information may not be correct. Even running a Better Business Bureau report may be unreliable, as it is possible to pay to have negative items removed. Engineering News Record is an excellent source.
3. Check referrals that were submitted on the bid.
4. Do a Google search on the company to look for any news. In fact, I like to set up Google alerts for all my vendors, this way if something pops up about them I will be notified right away and can take necessary steps if deemed needed.
5. Talk to people who have used them or worked with them before.
6. Google search them to see what comes up.
7. Check them against the US-banned contractor's list (https://www.dol.gov/agencies/ofccp/debarred-list).

There are two other members of the team that should be considered. They are not as common as an internal project manager but very important.

CONSTRUCTION CONTROLLER OR PROJECT CONTROLLER

A construction or project controller is a person who does not work on any of the projects but instead oversees all projects. They receive copies of all invoices, change orders, and track all project costs – by trade, by vendor. They are used to be the voice of all projects. By recording all vendor costs, they look for trends and patterns. They should be the first point of contact to ensure all invoices are paid. In order to keep independence, they are not a decision maker but can work together with project managers about decisions they make. They conduct vendor audits to ensure and may interact with Procurement on some of their findings.

CHANGE ORDER CLINICIAN

Another party that can be important is a change order clinician. This person is a decision-maker. They sit on the project team and represent end users. They get involved in the final walkthrough and sit on the change control board. Let's assume you are building a hospital, the clinician may be a nurse or doctor. They ensure that if a change order is approved, it will not affect the end product. They focus mainly on the function pillar.

CASE STUDY 1

Construction was underway at a large apartment complex. Due to some problems on construction and delivery of apartments on a timely basis, Audit was called in to do a review. The auditor realized that the contractor, JBK (not real name), was not their normal contractor and had not heard of the company being used. A review of the website revealed that they had only ever done residential construction. The auditor asked procurement to prove that the vendor had been vetted. The procurement officer said they would get that to them later in the day.

While waiting for the vetting documentation, the Auditor looked at the competitive bids that came in and noticed that the winning vendor was the lowest bidder. But something seemed off. When she compared the bids side by side, she noticed that the bidders were mathematically too similar. Every line item on the JBK was exactly 10% lower than the next lowest bidder. The next bid for every line item was 15% lower. She had a meeting to go to but decided she would stop by Procurement afterward. She gathered up her file and went off to the meeting.

The meeting ran over and by the time it was over, most people had left for the day. She knew the Procurement Officer often worked late so decided to see if she was still there. As she approached the desk, the auditor saw that the procurement officer was reviewing a bid from one of the normal vendors. As she got closer, she realized she was not reviewing it, she was creating it!

A further investigation revealed that the Procurement Officer had not sent the bids out for the apartment complex. Instead, she had JBK submit a bid and then she created competing bids so that JBK would win. She has used Excel to just plug in figures that were higher.

CASE STUDY 2

I was reviewing several bids that came in on a major infrastructure project. In this case, bids were sent out by mail, not electronically. I noticed that one of the bids went to a PO Box. This is not unheard of but raises concerns. Why not just send it to the office? Why have a PO Box? As I was reading the bid, more red flags emerged. I recognized the name of the bidder through one of my Google alerts. Further investigations show that he should not have been invited to bid. The PO Box was used as all inmates had PO boxes. Yes, the bidder was in jail, ironically, for charges of fraud and money laundering.

NOTE

1 The Real Deal, Construction Firm Indicted for MWBE fraud, November 2023.

Chapter 13

Common procurement risks

Choosing your vendors for a project entails certain uncertainties and risks. The vendor selection process for the organization needs to be well documented and enforced and these same processes should be transferred to the project management team. The vendor selection process should be written into the contract, as well. Traditionally, the vendors recommend other vendors, leaving to ponder: are they being recommended for their merit or for their relationship?

Commercial projects can last for years so it is important to ensure that the vendor will be on the project for the long haul. This requires that they are financially strong, established and (hopefully) lawsuit free. Contract negotiations alone can last months. Starting construction before the contract is signed is risky but not uncommon in construction. To protect the organization, the vendors should be selected as early as possible so that you have time for contract negotiations. Sometimes moving the start day is too expensive or the timeline is too tight to postpone the start while contracts can be finalized. An unsigned contract can result in higher-than-expected costs but worse; if an accident happens before contracts are signed, insurance companies may deny claims, assuming that insurance is already in place.

Organizations that do multiple projects a year tend to use the same vendors over and over. There is nothing wrong with this but to ensure fair pricing, bids should still be solicited. Additionally, the more comfortable the vendor becomes with the organization the less accurate their invoices may become. The error rate escalates the longer an organization is on there.

Additionally, if a vendor is doing multiple projects for the organization, dropping the vendor on one project can have costly repercussions on the other projects. It may lead to confusion as to which employees should be on which site and which should not. It also leads to confusion as to which costs are reimbursable for existing work and which should be denied for terminated work.

Before you work with a general contractor you will need to decide whether you want to use union labor. If you do want to use union, ensure that they

DOI: 10.1201/9781003461487-14

can secure workers to do the job. Additionally, when vetting vendors, it is important to know that they are not only qualified to do construction work but they have experience in the specific type of contract that matches the project. When construction activity slows you will often see vendors who do residential work bid on commercial projects; alas, though some skills overlap, they are not necessarily interchangeable. The more technically difficult the project, the more important this becomes. If workers need to be trained to work on the project, the responsibility of building the laborer's skill set should be on the contractor but I have often noted that it was not.

As mentioned earlier, many times the owner organization will outsource the procurement of the vendors to the architect-engineer, project leader, construction manager or general contractor. I have even seen projects where the owners were told they did not need to go to bid openings. This is relinquishing a bit too much control. At a minimum, someone from the organization should at least observe the bid opening. If that person is the auditor, remember, they cannot vote on the winning bidder. If asked for an opinion or vote, the auditor must abstain. Failure to do so will hinder independence.

Sadly, procurement is rife with fraud. Examples of procurement fraud are:

1. Price fixing (be careful, this is not the same as fixed pricing)
2. Bid rigging
3. Defective pricing
4. Fraud in needs determination
5. Fraud in development of work specifications
6. Fraud during solicitation
7. Split purchases
8. Upfront deposit frauds
9. Phantom (ghost) vendors
10. Other bidding fraud

PRICE FIXING

Price fixing is when competitors collude with one another to affect the price of a good or service needed for your project. There is a greater risk of this when you use the same vendors over and over. It is understandable that some vendors may have special expertise on the project, but you must proceed with care. Price fixing is a form of monopolistic trading. Auditors or project managers may become aware of price fixing when they notice that certain items have identical prices. Each company has bargaining power and write-ups so it would be extremely coincidental for the parties to have identical numbers. In a true scenario of job costing, all contractors would have unique costs due to expertise, labor, negotiations, and interpretations of the project and project specifications.

BID RIGGING

Bid rigging is a form of collusion to win a bid. It is a form of price fixing and market manipulation. It aims to get winning contracts to be assigned to the contractor at prices that are not representative of the work provided. In cases of kickbacks, these may come because of bid rigging. Due to the nature of construction bidding, bid rigging may occur between general contractor and sub-contractor. This will be hard for the owner organization to note if they are not present at that bid opening, or at a minimum, receive copies of the bids.

It might be possible to identify it during a construction audit if procurement is part of the scope. To look legitimate, the bid rigging payments may pass through the project via change orders. Change orders should always be part of the scope but due to the complexity of bid rigging schemes, it is advisable that they are rigorously audited. The reason is that change orders may be used as a conduit to provide kickbacks.

DEFECTIVE PRICING

Defective pricing is the submission of costs or pricing that is not true, to either gain an advantage of winning a bid or to inflate costs and get reimbursed more than was paid. Defective pricing may occur during the bidding phase or maybe during the payment reimbursement phase. If this is done on a government project (using Federal Acquisitions Regulations [FAR]) an adjustment to the contract price should be done even if the contract is already in force. The federal government would also be able to require any overpayments, interest on those overpayments, and possibly penalties. Add to that, criminal charges may also result. Defective Pricing with regard to government contracts falls under the prevue of the Truth in Negotiations Act. Punishment will all depend on whether intent can be proven. Misjudgments of estimates are not necessarily defective prices. Repercussions for a private contract would come down to contract wording for the project.

It is important to note that defective pricing may not be limited to just goods acquired for construction. It can also be done on labor, equipment rental rates and material – when we talk about payment testing, we will readdress this issue.

FRAUD IN NEEDS DETERMINATION

Fraud in needs determination occurs when a bidder deliberately underestimates the amount of material that is needed on your project. They do this to get in on a low bid. This is also a symptom of potential insider training. After the work begins, they will put in change orders for additional work or costs. If change orders subsequently get denied, the contractor may try to take shortcuts in other areas of the project; this will preserve cost but likely compromise quality. They will state site conditions as a need for the change. This is normally coupled with other frauds that we will discuss later.

FRAUD IN DEVELOPMENT OF WORK SPECIFICATIONS

Fraud in the development of work specifications involves budgeting for more material than is needed (that the contractor will use somewhere else) or developing work specifications and pricing out the needs at an unrealistic rate. This scheme may eventually unravel, especially if project managers or auditors do an inventory count on materials and find missing materials.

FRAUD DURING SOLICITATION

Another fraud has been found when auditing construction activity. For example, overinflated experiences. This would involve false reviews, misled resume activities and claiming to have licenses or qualifications that they do not actually have. I recall one project manager who was very excited during the presentation stage to tell us all about his schooling at MIT. He emphasized how they were superior in teaching engineering. We did some background checking and it showed he only attended MIT for one semester and it was not for engineering, it was for history. The due diligence of calling MIT did not take long and probably saved the project issues later on.

The opposite can also happen. This happens when companies deliberately omit to disclose any negative information to win a bid. Fraud related to financial strength especially before a bankruptcy, phoenix (a new company with the same directors is formed but is not subject to the former company's liabilities) or insolvency claim can be detrimental to a project. It could be argued that by winning the bid, they may be able to fix their financial issues; however, it is still fraud in the omission of information.

SPLIT PURCHASES

Split purchases happen when purchases for the projects are split into several different pieces so that the purchase will be approved by a person who would not have the signing authority for the whole purchase. Many times, we see this with change orders. We will discuss that in the change order chapter.

UPFRONT DEPOSIT FRAUD

Upfront deposit fraud occurs when the contractor charges a large deposit (more than 10% of the construction budget) and then leaves and does not show up to complete the work on the project. In some cases, the vendor will stay on but will charge for full cost of material and equipment without ever applying the credit for the deposit. Deposit fraud is more common with residential construction, but I have seen it on commercial projects as well. In theory, deposits should not be charged for normal tools and supplies. There may be a deposit for long lead time items such as generators or steel. In such a case, there needs to be a written agreement and controls around how to account for deposit and ensure that the contractor fulfills the work. It may be prudent to consider using an escrow agent or asking for segregated savings accounts to ensure money is used only on the project. The auditor should be sure to include verification that funds are held in escrow and test to ensure that withdrawals and payments are only for the project in question.

PHANTOM VENDORS

Phantom or fictitious vendors are not real entities but are used to send payment to, even though no goods were procured, or no services were provided. Controls to prevent this would be to ensure that the accounts payable department cannot add a vendor without correct supporting documentation. Usually, a fictitious vendor's role on the project is more service-oriented, as it is difficult to detect that services were not provided. Goods can be audited as they are tangible. Auditors should examine site access sheets to ensure the vendor has signed in to access the site for works invoiced. Some red flags include:

- Sequential invoice numbers that indicate no other customers are billed.
- Invoice amounts just below the purchasing authority of the approver.
- Companies without tax identifications.
- Companies without websites or physical addresses. It is recommended that in case of a website, auditor should access the site and ensure that the website indicates goods/services received are listed on the site. For example, if they are billing for nuclear safety education, is this a service marketed on their site.

OTHER BIDDING FRAUD

The above are examples of fraud seen over the years. It is important to question any indication that fraud exists on the project or during the procurement of vendors for the project. The above is not fully inclusive, as new frauds come out all the time.

Chapter 14

How project procurement can be different

Typically, with procurement, an in-house procurement team is used. One would submit a request telling procurement of what they need and when they need it by. Procurement will check their vendor list and contract the need out to a vendor or submit it for a public bid, asking vendors to bid on the project. These are generally sealed bids that a procurement officer will review or a group of persons involved will open and evaluate, choosing who is the preferred candidate.

This is not always the case when dealing with project procurement. Firstly, there is usually a team of people involved, mainly members of the project team. Some may be internal employees; some may be external to the company. With construction, generally the team will recommend vendors. These may be vendors the organization has never before worked with. They will suggest a vendor and highlight why this vendor is ideal for the project. They rarely are asked if there is a connection (financial or otherwise) between them and the referring vendor. They should be. It is recommended that the owner organization be extra diligent to ensure that there is no conflict between the suggesting party and the party nominated. The owner organization should be present at all bid openings.

The procurement policy for the project should be written and be the same if not stricter than the policy for internal procurement. Templated checklists may be used to capture relevant information from all bidders and to allow bidders to be compared on an even playing field. Checklists should include:

1. Name of vendors bidding
2. Date bids were received (sealed)
3. Amount bid
4. A line-by-line comparison of all bids
5. Votes for the winning bidder
6. Subjective comments or special consideration if they exist.

These checklists should be audited. Audit should ensure that bid information was correctly recorded, winning bidder was selected fairly and any

DOI: 10.1201/9781003461487-15

exemptions from policy are documented. They should further audit the contract and match it to the bids to make sure there have been no changes.

There are some red flags that audit should look for:

1. None of the known vendors of the organization were invited to bid.
2. Bids were limited and some 'well-known' vendors were not used.
3. Bids were returned very quickly (within a day or two of the bid going out to tender).
4. Scope of services on bidding document is very vague.
5. Adopting unreasonable pre-bid qualifications.
6. Bid does not equal contract.
7. Publication of bidding documents to only a small number of vendors.

Often, we will see sole-sourced contracts in construction. This is not an exemption in and of itself, but care should be taken to ensure that the contractor is indeed the only vendor who could do the work. Requirements that exist just to exclude vendors should be noted and questioned.

Selecting the correct vendor does not just rely on cost. The most important part is how cooperative they are in team situations. Past relationships, if tense, can be an issue. Once selected even the contracting changes. Normally a vendor contracts with the general contractor though we are now seeing a shift where contract is between the vendor and the architect. In either case this is what we refer to as a subcontractor.

Though you may come across the decision in other situations, of specific risk, is whether or not you want to use a union shop vendor or to pick an independent vendor and run the risk. Using union labor has positives and negatives. On a positive note, union labor:

- Provides rigorous training and creates an experienced labor pool.
- Creates a large talent pool.
- Provides internships so that new employees are supported by supervisors.
- Reduced the risk of union shops picketing the site (Trust me! The union rat is not cute!).

Non-union

- Lower cost
- Reduces the risk of walkouts and industrial chance
- Greater flexibility to 'crash' timeline
- No need to pay for apprentices
- Smaller labor pool

Whichever you choose, non-union or union, it should be the same that was used to cost out the project when asked for investment appraisal.

Contracting for the project is different than everyday organization procurement and there are times that during project procurement everyday organization procurement looks to purchase and build long-term relationships with the vendors. There may be contracts that offer a strategic pricing if a certain volume of spends. There may be customizations of projects. There may be billing arrangements so that the vendor is sending one invoice for all monthly orders. Project procurement may not be so straightforward. If the vendor is one that the contractor or project manager uses themselves, there are sometimes conflicts as to which contract gets the credit.

Chapter 15

Contracting

There are four main types of contracts used in construction services:

1. Lump Sum or Fixed Fee
2. Cost-Plus
3. GMax or GMP
4. Design-Build

FIXED FEE OR LUMP SUM

With a fixed fee or lump sum contract, the contractor agrees to oversee the contract and the work, pay all subcontractors and manage the contract all for a fixed amount that should not change. They agree that they understand the project and have examined the site to ensure that it is construction-ready and that nothing on-site should get in the way. They will agree on a payment schedule that is generally the contract sum (or lump sum) divided by the number of months the project should take. Fixed fee contracts are considered the easiest of the five types of contracts. Alas, they often will change the amount via change orders. We will discuss change orders later.

Many feel that fixed fee contracts don't need to be audited, as the price is fixed. This is not true. I have audited fixed fee contracts and found many exceptions, such as:

- Intangible items (such as insurance) not procured.
- Scope of work not completed as agreed.
- Items already in original scope charged for via change orders.
- Services contracted for not received.
- Payment to subcontractor not made so subcontractor bills owner directly.
- Payments charged exceed the contract amount.
- Billings continue past scheduled payments.
- Use of unskilled or unsupervised workers.

DOI: 10.1201/9781003461487-16

A derivative of fixed fee contracts is a percentage of completion contract. In this contract, instead of costs being the same for every month, the percentage of completion relies on how much work is done. So, if 25% of a $8 million contract is complete, the owner would be billed $2 million less whatever had been billed to this point.

COST-PLUS

Cost-plus contracts are very common. With a cost-plus contract, the project is charged for actual costs plus a percentage for profit. It is ideal for projects where there are too many unknowns on the project – especially design. The problem is budgeting for a cost-plus can be problematic with so many unknowns. There is no incentive for the contractor to save money as the more the cost, the higher they get in terms of the percentage of profit and overhead. A cost-plus contract should surely be audited to ensure that the costs charged match actual costs and to ensure that the overhead and profit amount is accurate.

Cost-plus contracts are usually used when the owner company feels that the budget they have set is too high and they anticipate that it could be done for less. Many government contracts rely on cost-plus contracts. When bidding for a cost-plus arrangement, emphasis should be based on skill and experience, rather than just lowest price. There may be incentives built into the contracts – such as completion ahead of time. If incentives were paid out, they should be audited to ensure that the incentive was met.

GMAX OR GMP

GMAX or GMP stands for guaranteed maximum contracts. A guaranteed maximum price has been designed to help allow for the problem of budgeting and letting payments skyrocket. The maximum price is called an upset price. These contracts may be called Contractor at Risk as the general contractor assumes the risk if cost is more than expected and exceeds the upset price. There may be incentives in these contracts as well.

The most common incentive we see with GMAX contracts is a Savings Incentive Clause. This clause states that if the final contract price comes in under the upset price, the owner agrees to split the difference with the contractor. Usually, the incentive split is 60/40. This is to encourage the contractor to look for cost savings and reward them for doing so. If a savings incentive clause has been paid out, audit should not assume the calculation is accurate. Audit should try to tie the figure in and/or discuss with project management the calculation.

You may be thinking, how complicated could that be? You simply match the amount paid to the upset price and you are done. Unfortunately, this gets complicated due to change orders or a discussion over what should be included in the upset price (should it include intangibles or indirect costs).

The calculation can be quite timely and calculated so often it is just negotiated. This is not the recommended calculation method. To avoid this, change orders need to be managed and organized so you can easily determine what causes rises or declines in the project costs.

DESIGN-BUILD

Just like the name implies design-build contract is when a contractor is selected that handles everything from the design of the project through to the build-out. This is done through one fixed price and all decisions are made directly by the contractor. It is imperative that all the design choices of the owner are made and laid out during the bidding process. It is costly and time-consuming, to make any changes after bidding. In design-build, the contractor is being left to manage it all – time, money, scope, function and quality. Owners need to be clear on what exactly they want. It does help eliminate or overlap some steps so it can be considered a faster way to do things. It is ideal for simpler projects where design decisions are less important.

Similar to design build are EPC contracts. EPC contracts tie engineering, procurement and construction into one contract. These are usually seen on large-scale and complex infrastructure projects. You will normally hear EPC and design-build contracts be called turn key contracts, as the owner hands over the specifications and then takes over again once the keys are handed over.

When identifying what type of contract you have, be careful not to determine what type of contract it is by looking at the title. Many times, contracts are modified and once the ratified agreements are in place, you may find that the new conditions have changed the type of contract you have. Look for key clauses as shown in Table 15.1.

Table 15.1 Standard clauses per contract type

Fixed Fee	Payment for the construction of Project 761-C shall be made according to the payment schedule set out in Appendix C, which stipulates $1,300,000 per month for a period of 16 months, subject to a retainage of up to 10% per payment.
Cost-Plus	Contractor shall receive as compensation a fee equal to ten percent (10%) of the Project Cost, which said term is defined herein below, incurred in the construction of the Project. The term 'Project Cost', as used herein, shall include any and all fees and expenses incurred in the course of construction of the Project, including all costs of labor, materials, subcontractor profit, expenses, allowances and change orders, whether such is paid by Contractor or Owner. The following items shall not be charged as Project Cost: Architectural and design fees paid by Owner, land procurement costs paid by Owner, bank fees paid by Owner, salaries of Contractor's management and supervisory personnel, expenses of Contractor's offices, Contractor's overhead and general expenses and Contractor's capital expenses.

(Continued)

Table 15.1 (Continued)

Gmax	ABC Construction Corp. has a contract to build an 18-story office block, and the agreement states that costs cannot exceed $25 million. ABC's profit is agreed at 15% of the contract's full price of $21 million. Additionally, ABC Construction is eligible for an incentive if the project is completed within nine months.
Design-Build	Design-Builder shall provide Total Project Design-Build Turnkey Services on the Project from inception to closeout. These services include planning, design, engineering, construction, project management and commissioning. In exchange for this, owner will pay the stipulated sum of $7.5 million.

Chapter 16

Contracts

STANDARD CONTRACTS

There are contracts which have been standardized by the industry and may be in use on many construction projects. Standard contracts are great to use and may take a lot of the guesswork out of forming a perfect contract. Some of the standard boards are:

1. American Institute of Architects.
2. Consensus Docs – a conglomerate of 20 organizations in the construction, architecture and engineering fields.
3. FIDIC – A set of agreed contracts used by over 100 countries, mostly European or the Middle East. The contracts are used globally on many projects.
4. Joint Contracts Tribunal (or JTC) which established standard building contracts for the United Kingdom.
5. NEC – New Engineering Contracts which were formed by ICE (Institution of Civil Engineers) in the 1980s.

The goal of standard contracts is to save time and money by avoiding lengthy negotiations. But they aren't without risks. They are generally negotiated contracts where the industry leaders get together with the contractors and negotiate favorable terms. Sadly though, most of these terms favor the contractor, not the project owner. We will talk about some of these differences and how to strengthen these contracts in a bit.

In the industry, if the owners handle most contracts in-house, they may be excellent attorneys but not quite experts in construction. It is common for the construction project to be contracted for using one of the standard templates and then modified to make everyone in agreement. It is often to add certain clauses and codicils from the owner. The problem is these clauses make sense from a legal risk perspective but not necessarily what is needed on a construction project. Often, we see industry language being used but

DOI: 10.1201/9781003461487-17

not everyone knows or understands the technology used. In the exercise of making a concrete contract, many times efforts fall short. The other issue is that some contracts are titled as one type but through amendments and footnotes it turns out that they are now defined as a different type of contract. I tell all my students never to rely on the heading of the contract but instead to read the words as seen in the table of the last chapter. That being said, if the wording of the contract no longer matches the title, it is worth noting, as the company may be operating thinking that they have one type of protection when, in fact, they do not. That would be your first finding.

Using standard contracts is advantageous because of the following reasons:

- Reduced cost and time for drafting and negotiating
- Easy familiarity with contract terms and conditions
- Higher confidence in contract validity and enforceability
- Less room for deviation and dispute
- Established body of case law for interpretation and guidance

But because standardized contracts were drafted and agreed upon by mostly contractors, there are disadvantages as well:

1. One size fits all mentality. We have already discussed that every project is unique, the contracts need to FIT the project.
2. The standardized **language** used in most contracts, often found toward the end, may not cover all necessary aspects. It is more about what it omits rather than what it contains. I talk about some of these in the following chapter.
3. Standardized contracts generally favor the contractor.

Consensus Docs came about in 2007 and it was a conglomerate of 20 organizations in architecture, engineering and construction. There were no owners represented in the conglomerate. The goal of consensus was to transform the construction industry by creating documents that are in the best interest of the project, NOT the owner. Some may argue that the project and the owner are synonymous, but they are not. The consensus Docs were designed to provide fairness and balance. In many respects they do. There are other standards other than Consensus as I mentioned above, but again they followed similar histories and were drafted by non-owners. Therefore, they have the same issues. I believe that standard contracts are good – as a starting point and if they can be carefully customized for the owner AND the project all the better. If the owner is doing their first construction project or their twenty-first project, addressing the contract at the beginning and end of the project (as lessons learned) then they can continue to protect themselves.

BUILDING A STRONGER CONTRACT

Whether you opt for a templated standard contract, a draft of your own, or the contractor's contract, there are some clauses that it is important to note and include. It may be wise to have a checklist that lets the auditor highlight and cite key phases, especially those that will be needed for the audit itself.

A good contract requires that all the details that can perceivably be an issue later in a project are agreed upon in advance and that the agreement is accurately reflected in the contract. Many agreements during the project may result in 'handshake deals.' Although a handshake deal is still binding, it is hard to audit, litigate or prove unless it is reduced to writing.

RIGHT TO AUDIT

The first clause that needs to be included and cited is the actual right to perform an audit and the right to get access to information needed. Many templated clauses allow for *reasonable* documentation. It normally does not state how long the right extends to. Many times, this is interpreted as three years from the transaction date. In many cases the audit may not start until after the project is complete. This would cause many transactions to fall outside the three-year time frame.

Let's look at the reasonable documentation component. Reasonable for whom? Reasonable for what? Do documents need to be original or copy? How long does the contractor have to turn things over? How long does contractor have to reimburse for any overcharges? One recommended clause would read:

> *Contractor grants the right to audit to Company A for a period of 60 months from completion of the project and shall have access to all original source documentation used directly and indirectly over the course of the project. In the event of any overpayment, contractor will agree to pay overpayment within 75 days and in the even that overpayments in excess of 5% shall be found, contractor shall split reimbursement for reasonable cost of the audit with Company A.*

An auditor may want to audit the subcontracts as well. Therefore, it should also be written into all subcontract agreements, as well. This right should be spelled out in the contractor contract so that if the auditor then receives feedback or refusal from the subcontractor there is some room for the auditor to defend the right to audit. Language for that might be:

> *As a result of audits being done on the project, we hereby request that contractor negotiate with the subcontractor and advise them of the owner's right to audit for up to 60 months past the construction*

end day. As a party to these negotiations, we hereby request that all requests from the owner company be obliged and adhered to. Said documentation should be delivered in an electronically readable format, if possible.

To facilitate any audits being done, it is preferred that data is delivered electronically so that Computer Aided Audit Techniques can be used. It is a battle during construction audits to get data this way. Add it into the contract as a forethought to ease audit efforts later.

DOCUMENT RETENTION AND DESTRUCTION

Many states require that documentation for construction lasts for the life of the asset constructed plus thirteen years. Many construction contracts require a lot less, usually six years. To prevent problems, owners should state in the contract that the documents should remain until (at least) 36 months after the final audit is completed. In addition, construction companies should not dispose of any documentation (nor should they charge for destruction). Instead, they should hand over all documentation to the owner. The owner can then take on responsibility for storing the documents or destroying them securely. This will be particularly important when destroying records that contain confidential information:

- Safety incidence reports
- Payroll records
- Blueprints (especially of secure facilities)
- Construction audit or construction fraud investigation reports
- Secure data information and data libraries.

Due to records and retention rules, we hereby require that the contractor hand over all documentation to owner in lieu of destruction of same.

RESPONSIBILITIES

The next item that should be included is the expected responsibilities of the parties under contract. This goes beyond just 'Contractor A agrees to build a 12-story office building for Owner A in exchange for $3 million dollars payable in equal amounts over 18 months.' The level of details are more minute items such as:

- Who will file for permits and other regulatory requirements?
- Who is in charge of security during working hours?
- What are working hours?
- Who is in charge of security after working hours?

- How will costs for security be allocated?
- What reports will be issued and when?
- What happens when changes need to be made?
- Must all changes be approved in advance? Who should the approval come from?

Some of the answers to these questions may seem like they can be answered in advance, or the answers are so obvious that they can be assumed. Allowing answers to be assumed is when trouble will start arising. For example, a project may be done and an employee not on the project asks for or approves a change because they are in a senior role at the organization. You may now be thinking that there is too much to answer all these questions, and you would be right. This is why contracts are as long as they are. And even then, there will still be gaps.

If construction projects are going to be ongoing at an organization they should have templates, but they should be living templates. That is, there should be a central repository for contracts but also templates can be changed for this project plus any future ones that come about. There should be a senior person at the organization who receives requests for contract changes and decides to amend just the current contract or to make the change across the board. Preferably this person should be from the Legal Department. As changes are made, this should be disseminated to the Project Management Office, should one exist.

As far as permits and variances are concerned, it makes sense for the architect or the general contractor to handle that as it requires submitting plans to the building department and possibly a need to explain the design. But again, this needs to be in the contract so that if permits are not filed or approved, it is easier to assign accountability.

SITE RULES

When specifying responsibilities on the contract, any specific site rules should be included. Examples of site rules that I have seen are:

- No smoking on-site – especially near flammable goods.
- Flammable goods need to be clearly marked, safely stored and inventoried.
- No alcohol or use of substances that may alter one's mental state.
- No foul language or vulgarity, especially if the site will be accessible by general public.
- Publication of fraud hotline, compliance hotline, and safety hotline – 'if you see something, say something' policy.
- Specific labeling of hard hat areas and publication of required safety equipment that must be used (steel-toed, rubber-soled boots, high-resolution vests, goggles, gloves, etc.)

- Site hours (especially if site is subject to curfew).
- Locking up equipment, flammables and tools.
- Clean site rules, such as disposal of food, waste and contaminants.
- Number of supervisors per workers, number of safety officers per workers and what to do in case of emergency.

DRUGS AND ALCOHOL USE

As we mentioned before, some of these rules or requirements may appear to be obvious, but don't let it be that way. Drugs and alcohol require special handling and an owner will want to protect themselves as much as they can. In the chapter on safety, I lay out the statistics around drug and alcohol use and it is an eye-opener when you consider that some workers are working on skyscrapers, balancing on small beams, hanging high above the streets below, working with explosives or operating heavy equipment. Mental impairment of any kind can mean life-threatening injuries occur and chaos ensues.

If injuries do occur, there will be questions that need to be answered – both from within the organization and outside. One of the questions bound to be asked was who caused the accident and were they under the influence of any substances at the time. You may not be able to – answer that unless you have a clause in the contract that allows you to do drug and alcohol testing. If the employee is union, they will not allow the test. Also, if the owner wants the right to remove anyone who looks impaired, that should also be written into the contract. The clause should state whether they will be removed with or without pay. The wording in the contract should state where the test will be done, who will do the test, when it will be done, and who will pay for the test.

In the case of implied or actual impairment of a worker, owner and it's representative have the right to remove said worker who shall be sent home without pay. Said employee shall submit to a drug screening test and may not return until LAB ABC has certified that there was no alcohol or drugs apparent in their system. If test should be negative, the cost of said test will be absorbed by owner, in the case of a positive test, vendor shall pay without reimbursement. The impaired worker may not return to work at the site without prior written authorization of owner company and evidence of a clean test.

CLEAN SITE

Clean site rules will mean different things to different people so if you require clean sites, the specifics should be spelled out: All tools are to be locked in a shed at the end of each shift, all work in progress to be left in area C, all rebar to be capped and piled, etc. It is akin to asking a teenager to clean their room. The standards of cleanliness will be different. If specifics are not included, it is impossible to determine compliance and hard to litigate. The standard is usually broom-swept. But this is usually left undefined.

The requirements may also be different at each phase of construction. For example, a hospital may require that at handover, the area is disinfected and sterilized. During construction the requirement will be less strict. Chances are that would not be the requirements if constructing a new garage.

DELAYS

Delays can happen for a variety of reasons:

- Supply chain interruptions
- Change in scope or user requirements
- Discovery of defects or site conditions
- Inspection delays
- Weather
- Delay in other dependencies
- Vendor availability

Some of these are predictable and are built into the schedule, others are not. The planning of the project is crucial to get an accurate time schedule but is only as accurate as the predictions you make and the tools you use. Delays are easy to predict if using any Building Information Modeling (BIM).

BIM is software that will bring plans to life – it will show you a finished product before it is even built. Using BIM can help predict clashes that would cause delays. It will virtually place laborers and equipment in the plans and determine if it will crash. In the absence of BIM, predictions can still be made based on patterns and known conditions. Projects in Detroit are more likely to be delayed due to snow than projects in Dubai. If schedules contain dependencies, it is easier to predict a delay earlier in the project and possibly even prevented. Timelines though seen as concrete can change. There is a technique called crashing the schedule that allows project managers to shift focus on a schedule to make delays to the timeline more predictable and less damaging. They do this by taking different paths to completion, reallocating resources, or paying and authorizing overtime.

Contractors can normally put in for delays that occur through no fault of their own. This allows them to collect money for delays or to qualify for incentives for completion on time. In respect to the delays, the contract should address:

- Initiatives for completion
- Criteria for what counts as a delay

- Reporting on delays
- Liquidating damages for delays in contractor causes
- Monthly reporting of time progress

Additionally, there can be other things that the owner may want, and failure may cause a financial hardship. Take for example, if you are building a commercial building such as a hotel, delays will result in lost income. If this is the case, the contract may contain a liquidating damage clause that asks for monetary remuneration if these goals are not met. Liquidating damages can cover any of the pillars of success we discussed earlier: time, cost, safety, quality, function and scope. I have also seen liquidated damages for projects being carbon neutral or able to achieve levels in LEED (Leadership in Energy and Environmental Design) qualifications.

This will become more and more common as companies embrace Environmental, Social, and Governance initiatives.

KEY PERFORMANCE INDICATORS

Key Performance Indicators (KPIs) are measurable goals the owner wants to achieve to measure the success of the project. These will be used to measure the performance of the contractor. Examples of KPIs on construction projects may include:

- Safety Record
  - Number of days without an accident
  - Number of accidents per vendor (keep in mind some vendors will have fewer accidents just as basis of the trade they are providing)
  - Actual working days versus available working days
  - Number of 'near misses'
  - Safety Training Completion
- Overtime Allowed
  - Number of workers on-site (actual vs promised)
- Percentage of Completion
  - Number of delays by subcontractor
  - Number of 'units' completed
- Number of Change Orders
  - Change orders by vendor
  - Change orders by owner
  - Change orders due to site conditions
- Variance from Budget
  - Savings from value engineering
  - Number of components completed on time or ahead of schedule.
  - Cost per square foot (actual vs bid)
  - Number of design changes needed

- Inspection Findings
    - Rework Rate (Percentage of work that has to be redone due to inspection issues)

Not only is it good to let the contractor know what success is, but it formalizes the goals and gives the contractor tangible goals to work for. Just make sure the KPIs are realistic.

With some of the standardized contracts, and even custom contracts, items are mentioned without being defined. Specifically, hard and soft costs. Hard costs are technically those costs that are part of the tangible asset; all costs included in labor, material and equipment. These costs are generally incurred in the construction phase and represent about 70% of the project costs. Soft costs are those costs that are not part of the tangible process. This would include permits, insurance, legal costs, payroll administration, banking fees and contract administration. This begs the question, what is not included? Unfortunately, there are items that fall as neither hard nor soft costs and they should be specified in the contract so instead of being debated when the time comes, it has already been decided. Examples of some of the middle-ground items are:

- Trailer costs for a temporary office at the site
- Training costs for specialty equipment
- Administrative salaries
- Demolition issues and price to ready the land

An agreement as to how these costs will be handled in advance will reduce conflict later. It is important that before the project negotiations start, the project team meets to figure out what the responsibilities in the project are.

PAYMENTS

Payment to other parties is an important part of what the contractor will do but can get confusing and leave one wondering if the wisest purchase or payment was made. There needs to be a definition in the contract as to

- how payment will be made,
- how it should be submitted for reimbursement/payment,
- how the payment is to be calculated, and
- what backup needs to be submitted with all payments.

Payment for labor should specify that prevailing wage should be paid and that the payment of wages is subject to audit. Prevailing wage calculations may change by jurisdiction and normally include

- a direct hourly reimbursement,
- overtime after 40 hours payable at time and a half,
- holiday pay, and
- all benefits.

Some jurisdictions further state that even if the contract specifies prevailing wage, an audit of such should be necessary or the owner can face penalty if prevailing wage is not paid. The other element with labor is specifying union vs non-union. Non-union labor is lower than union but may result in unexperienced workers, illegal workers or lack of benefits.

When the construction plan is being done, there may be a few items that require early purchasing or there are set-up costs that the contractor may face. This would entail advance payments and possibly deposits. These deposits and the repayment or return of the deposit should be spelled out. This helps set up a tracker system so that the owner can ensure future credit for that deposit. Many times the contractor may ask for a deposit for small equipment and tools. This request should be denied, as it would indicate a company that may not be equipped enough to handle the job.

Payments during a construction project are subject to a special process. Monthly, the contractor meets the owner and the architect, and they review the monthly invoice. This invoice before being reviewed is called a pencil copy. After the review, adjustments are made, and a final copy of the invoice is submitted for payment. This pencil copy process needs to be written into the contract.

Payments for equipment rentals need to be agreed to in advance – what rate will they use, what standard will they use. This most economical rate to use is monthly but unless it is specified, a contractor may use hourly as it will yield the greatest reimbursement.

Sources may mean Kelly, Equipment Watch or actual rental costs. These sources will give different rates; an agreed-upon guideline should be mentioned. Some rental rate guidebooks are based on national average, and geographical adjustments may need to be made. The guide you are using should instruct you on how to make that adjustment. The problem with actual is reimbursing the contractor for equipment they already own. Rates are further broken down into idle and used. Some may also include pipes, hoses or other disposable parts.

CHANGE ORDERS

No matter the project, planning it to 100% perfection is unlikely. This means that even with the best-laid plans, and attention to detail, changes will happen on a project. This can be as simple as changing paint color to having to do extra work to get a site ready for demolition, to a complete design change. Change happens! This means that change orders are bound to happen. Change orders are amendments to the project that will have an impact on the bottom line. Change orders may be issued by the owner, architect or contractor. Stringent change order procedures need to be maintained. We discuss this in more detail later, but as it relates to the contract, procedures should be highlighted in the contract. Procedures should be around approval, pricing, authorization and application to project costs. There should be two types of procedures: routine and emergency. Routine changes are changes that are being made that will affect the construction. Emergency change orders are urgent matters that need to be handled without taking time off to get approvals.

INSURANCE

We talk about insurance in the insurance chapter. The type of insurance that is agreed upon, as well as any limits, providers and the application of costs, needs to be discussed in the contract. This is to ensure that should a lapse in insurance occur, the responsibility for the insurance was laid out in advance and damages can be determined. If the owner wants to pre-discuss damages for lapse insurance, the contract is the place to do just that.

OUT-OF-STOCK ITEMS

There are times when material or furnishings may not be available when needed, forcing a change in that item. And while, a GE refrigerator versus a Samsung refrigerator may not seem like a big deal as a switch, it might be. Reasons why it would make a difference go back to agreements that may be in place with preferred vendors or sponsorships, consistency and other reasons. There needs to be parameters as to how replacement needs to be handled:

1. How does the owner get notified?
2. How are cost differences handled?
3. Does the owner need to approve before?
4. How much advanced notice does the owner get?

In the absence of specifying it in a contract, the usual implication is that replacements can be made with something of equal value. This is acceptable but sometimes value alone is not the only matter. Consider ordering a black car from a car dealer. There is a problem and the dealer has another car 'of equal value' but the color is hot pink. Is this an allowable replacement?

BAIL-OUT CLAUSE (EARLY TERMINATION)

The last thing that needs to be included in the contract is bail-out clauses for all parties. What happens at the end? Can one party break the contract under certain conditions? Does notice of cancellation need to be made? This is sometimes more important than the owner believes it is and turns out this one simple clause can mean millions of losses. The first two words to include in the contract are *Force Majeure*. This literally translates to unforeseen circumstances. Force Majeure is a clause in the contract that sets in the case of unforeseen activities either party can cancel without punishment. This is commonly known as an act of God or war clause. Consider that you have started a construction project and a hurricane comes through the area. If the damage is severe enough, the company may want to cancel the contract. A force majeure clause allows just that.

There are times when a construction contract may be ambiguous or otherwise requires debating terms on a contract. The contract should state what happens in this case. Most projects will call for arbitration or litigation. If the owner wants to opt for this, they should write it in. Be careful on contracts that name who the arbitrator will be. This should be a mutual decision so that you can ensure as much independence as possible. Before signing a contract, you want to check where disputes must be resolved: the site of the property, the site of the owner's executive headquarters or the site of the contractor's place of incorporation. This can help the owner decide the costs of having to defend an issue.

CONTRACT AS A RISKS

Even a well-written contract provides a level of risk, especially when what you write in the contract is not what you meant. Most construction contracts with amendments, riders and changes can easily become over 100 pages in length, it is long to write, written in legalese, hard to read and often interpreted differently by different readers. Additionally, many times what is written in the contract is assumed but not actually in there. Lastly, there are many reviews done and through these reviews individual changes get made. If construction is going to be a repeat item in the organization, it is best to get all in one room, come up with template contracts and use them. This will not eliminate all risks but will allow more control over what gets executed in its final form.

Early in my career, I had a contract where the person did not know if a word written on the contract was an 'and' or an 'or' so they put 'and/or' with the intention of getting clarification and fixing it later. Alas, no clarification was ever received. This resulted in a clause that stated *fee would be as speculated by FAR regulation x.y* and/or 5%. The construction company accounts payable clerk read it as 'and,' the owner read it as 'or.' The contractor wound up collecting fees, twice what was intended. The owner did not correct it as they treated it as 'or' when auditing the invoices. They felt if it went to negotiation, surely the negotiator would see reading it as 'and' would result in double billing. Well, it went to negotiation and because the owner typed up the contract, they ruled in favor of the contractor. The result of the error cost the owner several million dollars in excess fees.

The current processes for reading and interpreting contracts are usually ignored until a dispute arises. An auditor's first step is to read the contract, outline it and be able to highlight key clauses. I recommend creating a checklist of the below information and citing it in the contract so that auditors can easily find clauses that they may need when auditing the contract. Key clauses that should be highlighted are:

1. Dates the contract starts and ends
2. Stipulations that must be met before construction is to start
3. Agreed payment terms
4. Written bonus clauses
5. Scope of contract
6. Special stipulations
7. Any upset pricing (maximum amounts to charge)
8. Any specific exclusions
9. Milestones
10. Signatures
11. Agreed scope (This should be reconciled against the investment decision and changes should be noted.)

Unfortunately, there are many modifications and amendments to the contract and it may be difficult to find which is the correct version to use. In such a case, it is helpful to write the clause with the original wording and then the amended clause. Large deviations should be explained by the project manager. Also look for the date of the amendments (if possible) and ensure all amendments were made before the contract was signed. Amendments made after the signing should be investigated, as this can be erroneous or fraudulent.

The reason to look for signatures is many times construction starts but there are still some items left in negotiation. As an auditor, it should be noted if work commences before the contract is signed. This is especially problematic when the fixed fee or the upset price is still being negotiated. Besides taking away an advantage at the negotiating table, what happens if the upset price is reached before the contract is signed? I have seen some contracts where negotiations take months, and in a few cases, years.

It is recommended that an interview is performed with certain people (such as the project manager and the contractor) at separate times to understand what the contracts should say. There usually are discrepancies. These discrepancies should be checked back to the contract, to determine who was correct and then the auditor will need to assess the risk of these discrepancies against project success. If the risk is high, an immediate escalation to senior management or senior audit management is recommended. It may even be wise to loop in a member of Legal, as well.

When reviewing the contract, the auditor needs to look for areas that contain assumptions or implications and highlight these. When two clauses contradict one another, there will be issues. The sooner you can find them and establish the correct interpretation the better. It may require an amendment or rider to the contract which is why it is wise to include Legal in the discussion.

Cost-plus contracts contain room for error and zero incentive to bargain shop. They get paid a fee based on the amount of the cost. The more they spend, the higher the fee earned. This is not to say that cost plus should not be used. If designs are not decided on you run the risk that a fixed price is used instead and the contractor overestimates for the unknown. Also, in a time when construction costs are on a decline, cost plus allows you to take advantage of that.

Goldplating is a risk with cost-plus contracts. Goldplating occurs when a contractor intentionally gives extra over what was initially requested. This is done with the purpose of increasing the cost of the contract. This is why the GMAX contract came to be. An example of goldplating would be you order Sony 55-inch TVs for the lobbies and you get (and are charged for) 65-inch TVs. Goldplating is similar to scope creep, but the two are not interchangeable terms. Scope creep can be initiated by any stakeholder in the project, usually the client. Goldplating is usually initiated by the project manager.

CONTRACTS AS A CONTROL

A well-worded contract is the key to a successful project. Before choosing to use a standardized contract, the organization needs to decide if they have the expertise to protect themselves when writing the contract. As we discussed, procurement is different in construction projects, in that matter so are construction contracts. An organization may have a superb Legal team but construction is not their strength. They may review terms that the Legal department may be unfamiliar with. They may talk about project flow that Legal may never have experienced. By tailoring the contract to the specific needs of the project, it's possible to exert a high degree of control over how the project is carried out. If management does not feel that internal Counsel can handle a construction contract, there are many externals that can be consulted.

Legal may be familiar with problems that the organization has seen in the past. By knowing these, they can prevent the same problems from reoccurring by plugging specifics into the contract. The normal areas where specifications occur, using fall in the areas of:

1. Change control procedures. Change control procedures may be detailed to talk about approvals, pre-approved procedures, documentation requirements and notice periods. Prior projects that noted scope creep or gold plating may be one reason to add these modifications.
2. Risk allocation. Prior projects may highlight weaknesses in the organization – insurable losses, site conditions, overtime, weather, etc. By carefully wording the contract you can disperse that risk with the contractor or at least share in the risk. This is why many contracts charge a penalty for late delivery.
3. Cost and type of contracts. Organizations may want to opt for a fixed fee contract specifically to control cost overruns or avoid surprises due to hidden site conditions; the type of contract used can help this. Remember a fixed fee contract, as mentioned before, is a contractor at risk contract; therefore, this can be wise if they feel there may be risk about initial assessments and needs.
4. Dispute resolution. An organization may predict that there may be disputes on the contract. This may require that they send executives or Legal staff to another country to settle any disputes. By specifying the jurisdiction, the organization may be able to prevent costly legal and/or travel costs.

After the contract is signed, the executives and Legal should meet with the internal construction team or any decision-makers on the project. The problem we often see is that the contract protects the organization but the individuals managing the contract may not realize that the clauses are there.

Many decisions on the project are quick and may involve oral agreements. The project manager is trying to stay friendly with the contractor. Their actions sometimes cancel the controls that the Legal department carefully put in place to avoid the situation. This is not the fault of the internal person but by the nature of the agreement, the project manager is at a disadvantage. They are looking at all the bits and pieces of the project and walking a tightrope trying to keep the organization and the contractors happy.

An organization that writes their own contracts can experience and benefit from setting out clear expectations and the contractor benefits from this as well. The expectations encourage more open and honest billings. Clear scopes and specific timelines help the construction team stay on track and work toward unified goals.

Lessons learned at the end of every project can indicate where contracts need strengthening. Immediate adjustments should be made to the contracts so that they are not forgotten about or seen as a one-off problem.

Chapter 17

Earned value management

Earned Value Management (EVM) is a project management tool that helps one measure performance and progress on a project. It can help measure three of the six pillars of project success: **scope, time and costs**. It helps manage a project by providing insight into what has already been achieved, what it has cost to achieve this, and whether everything is progressing in such a way that cost and schedule goals will be met.

EVM allows you to answer some important questions on the project that executive management should know. Answering these questions in your audit reports will help you be an **audit hero**. Here are some of the questions you can answer:

- Are we currently on budget?
- Are we currently on schedule?
- Are we getting value for our money so far?
- What will this final project cost?
- How much more will we need to spend?
- Will the project come in on budget?
- How much are delays costing me?

Questions audit management may have can be answered using these formulas. Questions treasury management may have can be answered using these formulas. Keep it simple, when reporting this. Instead of saying 'Budget at Completion will be $35 million,' use easier household terms like 'The project will be $5 million over budget.'

I suggest that project management track EVM as they go along. In lieu of that the project auditor should. It is easy to automate the calculations. The formulas are summarized at the end of the chapter. Due to the ease of calculations, I have helped clients include these on the month-end project reports. It can be automated so that project management need only print the report and the calculations are done. If doing this, put a disclosure that formulas are subject to audit.

DOI: 10.1201/9781003461487-18

However, you will see that the formulas intertwine and that the answer for one may feed the answer to another. Because of that, I have broken the formulas into individuals first so you can see how they interact.

BAC

BAC is the budget at completion. This is the amount the investment committee has set aside for the completion of the project. It is not a formula you would be expected to calculate but it will be needed to calculate many of the other formulas. It answers the question – **How much is the project planned to cost?**

Even though this number is right there on the investment appraisal, foot the line items and ensure that this figure is commensurate with the appraisal amount. Often, I have found hidden buffers in this amount to compare with usual project experience. This is not the place for that buffer. It should be part of the contingency amount. The reason for this is human nature. If you tell someone they can spend $150 on something and you know they will go over budget, if you add a buffer in and tell them they can spend $175 – which will they spend?

PV

PV is the planned value of your project (PV = BAC / planned months * time invested). Planned value takes the total cost of the project (or BAC) divided by the term of the project times the duration of the project to date. So, if building an office building for 18 months at a cost of 18 million, at the end of two months the planned value would be $18,000,000/18 * 2 = $2,000,000. This answers the question – **Where should the project be at this stage?**

EV

EV is earned value. Earned value is how much the project has earned at this stage of completion. This is difficult to determine as you need to know the percentage of the project done. Fortunately, most construction invoices tell you know much is done as a percentage. The formula for earned value is BAC * percentage complete. This answers the question – **How much of the project has been accomplished?** Though this question is helpful, it is often used to just frame the rest of an analysis on project progression.

AC

AC is the actual cost. This number is not calculated but simply reflects how much has been paid out on a project. This is what has been added to Assets in the Course of Construction – for this project. I recommend auditing the transactions in the account first. It should be a two-way audit:

- Have project costs been recorded in the account of another project?
- Have costs for another project been logged to this project account?

To make a project look like it is progressing well, sometimes costs are not recorded in a timely fashion. This should be audited and if a slowdown is noted, ensure that there are no outstanding monthly bills. You can look for past trend versus current trend and see if there is a lag. There can be other reasons for the lag but in the least it should be investigated. It answers the question – **How much has the project cost us so far?**

SPI

SPI is the schedule performance index. This figure determines if you are on schedule or behind schedule. It is calculated as EV divided by PV.

- Any number less than 1 shows that the project is behind schedule.
- An SPI of 1 means the project is on schedule.
- An SPI of greater than one means the project is ahead of schedule. This is the preferred situation. But be careful. SPI should not be used as a stand-alone number. Instead, you need to graph SPI over time and see if it is trending in the right direction (Figure 17.1).

There are many things that can get SPI trending in the right direction:

Dynamics of the team: A team of new employees is still under pressure to figure out how to do their job without tripping on other members. They also need to determine other logistics – where are needed materials, where are needed tools, where does one sign in, etc. Also, we have a tendency not to ask for help at the beginning, to show expertise. Similar to the learning curve, as time goes on and the team gets to know one another, the work goes faster.

Learning curve – the ability to do repetitive tasks quicker and quicker over time because you are learning how to do it. Think about tying your shoe. As a child this took a minute or more as you would have to think about steps. By now, you no longer have to think, you just do it.

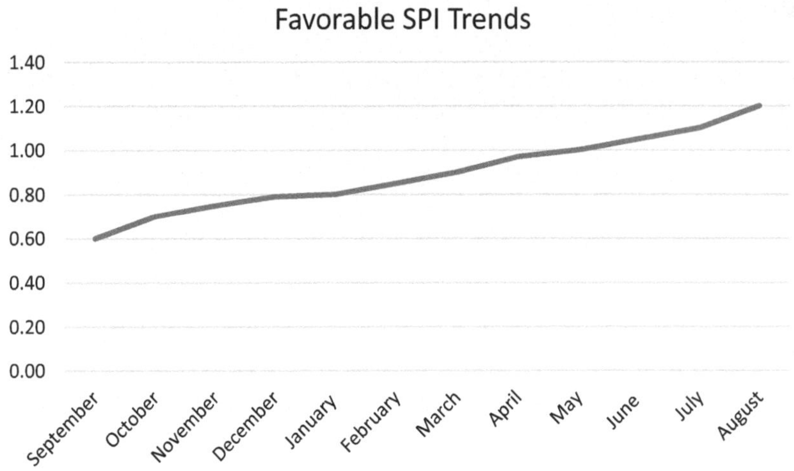

Figure 17.1 Favorable SPI trend.

Schedule management – There are a lot of things that can be done with a schedule and management can rearrange tasks, transfer labor to lagging items or change scope. There are other tricks up the sleeve of the project manager and a good project manager will be creative in getting a failing schedule back on track.

Favorable work conditions – just like weather can hamper progress on a project, an unexpected spell of good weather can help it along. A good project manager will take advantage of favorable weather but doing tasks that are more reliant on weather. Painting is quicker to dry on sunny days.

SPI answers the question – **Is the project progressing on time?**

SV

SV is schedule variance. It is the way to measure the cost of falling behind. It is impactful to say in an audit report that a project is behind schedule, but when you can monetize that – **wow!** To calculate schedule variance, subtract planned value from earned value. That will answer the question – **How much is the delay costing per day?** Keep in mind that this is only the schedule and project costs. If there are opportunity costs, such as lost revenue, this will not be captured in this equation.

CPI

CPI is Cost Performance Index. It is calculated as earned value divided by actual costs. It measures project performance and efficiency.

- The goal is to have a CPI less than 1. This means that the project is on or under budget.
- If the project has a CPI greater than 1, it is under budget.
- A CPI of 1 is perfectly on budget.

As mentioned above, it is still important to understand that CPI may be unnaturally increased if actual costs have been purposely delayed. It answers the question – **If we continue at this pace, will the project come in on or under budget?** or it is sometimes considered: **How much I am earning for every dollar spent?**

Similar to SPI, you don't want to look at CPI at a single point of time, instead you want to measure the trend and see if efficiencies are happening (Figure 17.2).

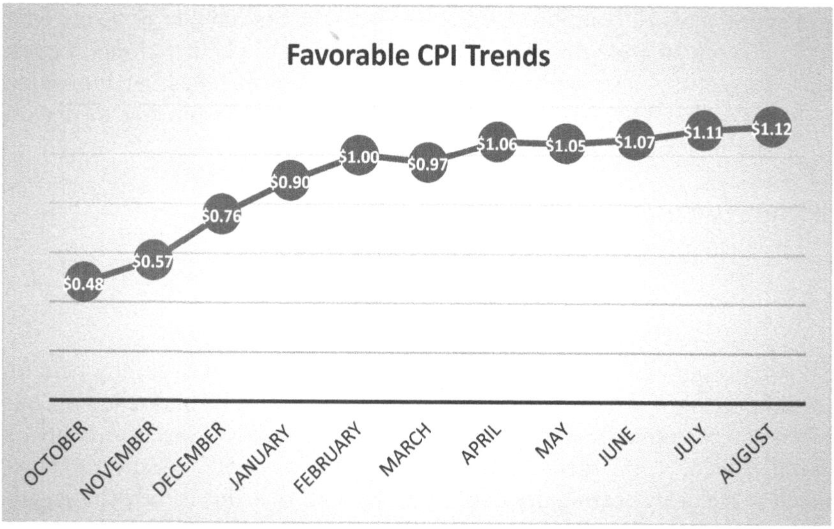

Figure 17.2 Favorable CPI trend.

ETC

ETC is the estimate to completion. ETC is calculated as BAC minus EV. This makes an assumption that future performance will be in accordance with plan and efficiency. The final calculation answers the question – **how much more will need to be paid out?** This would be a great number for Treasury Management and Project Management to have as they can ensure that if the budget is over budget, they will be able to access the excess funds before committing to another project. Additionally, if funds are being paid in another currency, it gives Treasury Management a chance to hedge funds.

EAC

EAC is the Estimate at completion. It can be calculated in one of three ways.

1. BAC divided by CPI
2. AC plus ETC
3. AC plus BAC minus EV

It answers the question – **How much will the project cost us in the end?** This is a helpful number for Treasury Management and Strategic Planning.

TCPI

TCPI is the To Complete Performance Indicator. It is a forecast of the budget to the end of project. It determines if the project should still come in at or under budget. It can be calculated using the following formula:

- (Budget – Earned Value)/(Budget – Actual Cost)

It answers the question – **How effective does the project have to be from now until completion to come in on budget?**

VAC

VAC is variance at completion. It is calculated as BAC – EAC. It answers the question – **how far from budget will the project come in at?** A negative number means it is over budget.

Keep in mind that these formulas do not consider lost opportunity costs, nor do they consider change orders – this is why change orders should be recorded separately.

These formulas will help add value to your audit. Creating a spreadsheet that will update all this as data becomes available will be helpful. These formulas have been summarized for you below (Table 17.1).

Table 17.1 Earned value management formulas

Formula	*Formula name*	*Formula*	*Answers*
BAC	Budget at Completion	None	How much is the project planned to cost?
PV	Planned Value	BAC * Percent planned to be complete	Where should the project be at this stage?
EV	Earned Value	BAC * Actual % complete	How much of the project has been accomplished?
AC	Actual Cost	None	How much has it cost so far?
SPI	Schedule Performance Index	EV/PV	Is the project progressing on time?
SV	Schedule Variance	EV – PV	How much is the delay costing?
CV	Cost Variance	EV – AC	How far off budget is the project?
CPI	Cost Performance Index	EV/AC	If we continue at this rate, will the project come in on or under budget?
ETC	Estimate to Complete	• EAC – AC	How much more will need to be paid out?
EAC	Estimate at Completion	• BAC/CPI • AC +ETC • AC + BAC – EV	How much will the project cost us in the end?
TCPI	To Complete performance index	(BAC – EV)/(BAC – AC)	How effective does the project have to be from now until completion to come in on budget?
VAC	Variance at Completion	BAC – EAC	How far from budget will the project cost?

Chapter 18

Inventory controls

Inventory control for tools and materials on a construction site is crucial to prevent loss or theft and ensure efficient operations. It is important to keep abreast of what is on hand and what is needed. Many times, construction projects work using a just-in-time mentality, but in times of short supplies or long lead times, they may resort to stocking material. The storage of inventory should be close to or on-site, locked and secured, and coordinated.

Theft of material is common in the construction industry due to the ease of selling tools on a second market and the inability to track material or equipment that leaves the site. If someone steals a hammer, it is improbable that you will note that hammer as out of place and realize it was stolen. They generally do not have any serial numbers on them, they all look the same, they are small and easy to hide. Many times, the theft occurs by placing the stolen goods in the back of an open van, truck or backpack. Some will even hang it off their toolbelt and walk away.

Some practical tips for controlling inventory and inventory costs include:

- A central, lockable location on-site where tools are locked and not accessible by the general public. For larger pieces of equipment (bulldozers, forklifts, dump trucks, piledrivers, etc.) they should be parked in a central location and if possible the wheels locked. A good foreman will park equipment in such a way that missing equipment is quick to be noticed. For example, if you park all the equipment in a circle, one missing piece of equipment will be obvious. Keys should be kept safely in a secure place. Do not leave keys in the vehicle!
- For bigger items or more restrictive sites, a central location offsite that is easily accessible to the site may be used. In city areas, space is limited, and it may be necessary to keep some equipment or material off-site. This is a good solution, but it should be close enough to the site where a truck can pick up what is needed and bring it back without too much delay. The auditor should visit the off-site location (if allowed) and verify that equipment and material are there and segregated by project.
- Delivery of material is audited to ensure all material was delivered to the site or designated off-site location. As part of the invoice review

DOI: 10.1201/9781003461487-19

process, criteria should be made to verify the delivery address is where the project is located. If a project number is noted on the invoice, verification should be made that it is the project being audited.

- A central person or persons who have access to locked sheds where material and equipment are to be kept. This limits how many people have access and allows for proper delegation and tracking of material and tools. There should be documentation showing which tool was given to which employee and then noting when it is returned. This should be done for equipment keys, as well. Keys should not be taken home. Keys handed in should be in a locked cabinet or container. There is an exception – if the site is under a severe weather threat, the nearest operator should take a key home with them and leave a backup behind. This is in case the weather event creates a need to move, brace, reposition or test the equipment (mostly this is cranes) and they cannot get to the key location. If there are no duplicates, the key should be kept on-site.
- Lock up everything possible when the site is closed or after distributing tools and material needed for the day. This is particularly important if the site may be closed the next day for severe weather. In high wind conditions or adverse weather conditions, material may be damaged or may result in a hazard if picked up in the wind. Quickrete can be rendered unusable if it gets wet. Anything that is not locked away may be subject to theft by contractors, employees or even passersby. There should be a limited store of common items that are on hand in case of emergency: hard hats, safety vests, small hardware, small tools, safety glasses, gloves, etc. This store is generally located near the exit to the site, though if the site covers a large geographical range, it is possible to have multiple stores.
- Limit the time flammables stay on-site. Fire is a serious risk on construction projects and the longer the flammables are accessible, the more you increase the risk of a fire disaster. Flammables should be kept off-site until needed. Additionally, flammables should be clearly labeled as such. If possible, they should be in a controlled and safe area tucked away from other material, dangerous vibrations and areas where fallen objects are a risk. The area should be a no-smoking zone, free of any open flames and clearly labeled. Anyone caught smoking near flammables should be noted on the Daily Foreman's report.
- Regular audits, scheduled and surprise, should be done to ensure that equipment counts reconcile with what is on hand. This may be a part of the foreman's responsibility or can be assigned to someone more independent of the process. Reconciliations should be signed and dated. Audit should inventory the equipment inventory reconciliations, yet still perform their own count. If the auditor counts a higher number in inventory than what is recorded, they should inquire to see if at any point the project was charged for lost or stolen material.

- Use of electronic systems. If using BIM or other software, tracking material electronically is possible. When using BIM, you can track each piece of wood, if you want. This was actually handy on one project I worked on. There was a recall of some of the equipment used on a University Athletics field. Using BIM we were able to identify where the equipment was installed and were able to quickly replace it. Some workers complain that scanning each piece of material is time-consuming and slows down progress. This is a valid argument, and the project team should discuss and determine if the slowdown is worth the risk. If the material was not tracked, it may have resulted in having to replace all the equipment and going backward. If electronic systems are not available, there should be at least a legacy system used to track what is on hand, what is needed, what should be ordered, and estimates of when they will be needed.
- Well-communicated schedules and tasks. Knowing what material will be needed on a day can be influential in ensuring that fewer trips need to be made to a central depot and that materials are available as they are needed. In a well-controlled schedule, project management should have created work breakdown schedules which show tasks for two-week time periods. By adhering to the work breakdown schedule the foreman should know exactly what is needed and where it should go. Granted there will be items that come up as surprises, but these should be more the exception than the rule.
- Identify tools as those belonging to a contractor or specific project. As I mentioned in the introduction of this chapter, stolen tools are hard to identify if they are taken off a site, a hammer looks like any of a million hammers on the site. However, if these can be labeled, engraved or tagged with colorful asset tags, it can be a deterrence for anyone looking to try and remove the property from the premises.
- Awareness and training should be part of the theft deterrence measures. All employees on the site should be on the lookout for stolen goods and materials or any suspicions of the same. They should observe if any particular employee asks for more tools or equipment than they are using or can use in a given day unless they are assigned to ready the site. Additionally, there should be a hotline or a trusted supervisor they can report suspicions to.
- All material should be delivered to the same delivery address(es) and the auditor should gather invoices and check the delivery addresses. Any exceptions should be investigated.

Controlling theft of supplies and material is important as the contractor will likely charge the lost items as a change order or as a direct cost during a cost plus or Gmax contract.

- Should the change order be approved?
- What does the contract say about theft of material?

- Is there insurance in place for builder's risk?
- What would be the impact of filing an insurance claim?
- Who pays for increased insurance premiums?
- Can the contractor continue without waiting for an insurance claim?
- If a claim is paid, did the project get credited?
- Is the cost of missing material a direct cost or an indirect cost (depends on the contract)?
- If material, how soon can it be replaced?
- How much will the theft slow progress?

As you can see from this line of questioning, theft of goods and materials can have long-reaching effects.

Keep controls basic: Lights, cameras and many sets of eyes are the main ingredients.

Chapter 19

Safety and site rules

Safety on a site is a big concern. There is a lot of equipment being used, a lot of chaos and the need to be focused at all times. Safety may be the first priority and may trump all other factors – money, scope, function, quality, etc. Some sites will even advertise how many days the site has been accident free. Several factors come into play that will help mitigate the risk of people getting hurt:

1. All workers (including site auditors) have been trained in at least the OSHA site safety course. This is a 10-hour course on Construction Safety and includes training and testing on-site clothing, safety features, how to use certain equipment, fall safety and height safety. This course can be done online and should take less than 12 hours. As part of the audit, auditors should be looking to ensure that workers can provide proof of OSHA training. If this is being done outside the USA, many countries have an OSHA equivalent.
2. Site safety personnel – For every 50 people on the site, there should be a first aid kit and a site safety employee. The site safety employee needs to be on for every minute that workers or visitors are present on site. This is sometimes a great way to not pay for overtime claims that may appear fraudulent or erroneous. Site safety personnel should be trained and, in this case, the 10-hour course is not enough. There is a more thorough 30-hour course that should be taken. Depending on the jurisdiction they may need to be a licensed paramedic or CPR professional. The Site Safety person may or may not be entitled to paid overtime (many are salaried).

   Of course, continuing education is also important. Auditors should check with local jurisdictions about requirements and should test that these requirements (at a minimum) are being met. (Same applies for general safety and number 1 above.) The contract should be referenced, as an owner may feel that one-to-fifty ratio is inadequate and they will want more safety officers. This is acceptable but the contract should not call for more than a one-to-fifty ratio.

DOI: 10.1201/9781003461487-20

3. Proper footwear, hard hats, safety goggles and high resolution are worn, and additional equipment is available should workers lose, damage, forget or need extra equipment. There should also be additional equipment on site in case visitors come. In more public sites (such as hospitals, education or residential facilities) clearly labeled equipment (labeled vests, hard hats or identification lanyards) should be worn so that workers are clearly and easily identifiable.

   Of course, then you need to balance on a tightrope and make sure that identification controls do not impair safety – i.e. a lanyard can get stuck in equipment. I have been often asked if steel-toed shoes are required. This depends on the type of construction and local regulations. Auditors can pose the question to the local zoning board or health department to find out more. Some jurisdictions will not allow steel-toed as it increases the risk of amputation, some require it and accept the risk of amputation.

   There are other features on safety boots other than just steel-toed. Some are waterproof, which may be required for outdoor work, some are puncture resistant, some are ankle supported and some are extra thick rubber sole for electrical work. There may even be requirements stating how far up the leg should the shoe be.

   Some require easy off, as well (a zipper up the side in case the shoe has to be quickly removed). The best shoe for the job being done should be what is required.

   Since shoes need to fit right, generally these are self-supplied by workers, but they may get a stipend should they need new pairs or to replace boots at certain intervals. When walking a site, the auditor should note any workers wearing shoes that appear to be worn out or damaged. Shoes with toes that are duct taped should not be worn.

   Hard hats should be required on sites but the color may be stipulated by local law. Generally, the differences are based on role – supervisor/worker. There may be requirements that stickers or markings be removed and that hats should not be used to express political views.
4. Correct signage including areas where trip hazards are hidden or prevalent. For example, if building a staircase and the banister is not yet attached or risers are not attached, a sign warning people not to use the staircase is wise. It is better if this area is cordoned off for people who may not be paying attachment.

   You might think common sense would prevail, but common sense should not be relied on as a control. Additionally, realize that sometimes on a site, workers are carrying large or heavy items that may block their vision. Human nature being what it is, the more comfortable people get doing stuff the more relaxed they are, and this works against safety risk.
5. Mandatory or suspicious activity drug testing – We will broach this subject again but being able to do drug or alcohol testing is important.

In 2021, The Insurance Factory, published a report on alcohol in UK Construction and it came up with the following results after interviewing 1300 construction workers:

- 59% are concerned about the effects of drugs and alcohol in the industry.
- 65% have never undergone a test for drugs or alcohol.
- 39% believe the issue of drugs or alcohol could be better addressed by their employer.
- 25% agreed that drugs or alcohol impacted them at work through tiredness.
- 23% agreed that it impacted them by reducing their attention span.
- 19% agreed that the effects of drugs or alcohol made them less productive.[1]

A recent study showed that the most popular profession of drug-related overdoses in New York was construction workers. The reason for this is many construction workers do not get sick pay (unless unionized, and even then, it is limited), leaving them in a scenario of no work/no pay. In order to work and get paid they will take (prescribed) painkillers and some have eventually become addicted.

6. Long Covid is having an impact on-site safety. Long Covid can make a person unable to concentrate and tire easily. Long Covid can take 18 months or more to recover from so many laborers cannot afford that. Afraid that they will not get paid or that the employer will not let them back, they may not report that they have Long Covid.

There is currently a shortage of skilled workers. This greatly increases the risk that the workers on site are illegal workers, trafficked workers, non-union workers or ineligible for work based on other reasons. In order to legitimize these workers, the contractor will pay them prevailing wage on paper but pay them less via check. To verify the amount contractors are paying employees, you can ask for the cash disbursement journals, reports of bank transfers, or interview workers at random to ask for proof and to verify the amount paid.

NOTE

1 The Insurance Factory (2021). 'Drug and alcohol abuse in the UK construction industry'.
https://www.insurancefactory.co.uk/news/April-2020/Drug-and-alcohol-abuse-in-the-UK-construction-indu

Chapter 20

Daily foreman reports

Foremen have many tasks on their plate everyday:

- Overseeing daily operations
- Coordinating tasks, vendors, visitors and schedules
- Managing budget
- Ensuring quality work is carried out
- Protecting the site and employees from hazards
- Reporting on progress
- Hiring equipment
- Delegating tasks and responsibilities
- Supervision

We are going to talk about reporting on progress. There are various reports that the foreman may prepare but the one of importance for the owner of the project is the daily foreman's report. This report is generated for every day of the project life cycle, even days when the site is closed. Communication among project stakeholders – from the owner and construction manager to the engineers and contractors – becomes smoother when they have a single source of truth as a guide. This report can do exactly that!

The report does not need to be overly complicated but should include the basics:

- Date
- Day of the week
- Site name
- Number of people on-site, workers and visitors
- Equipment used on the day
- A brief overview of what was done
- Incidents on the site
- Weather for the day
- Condition of parameter fencing
- Hours the site was accessed
- Photographs if necessary

DOI: 10.1201/9781003461487-21

It is important that one is kept for every day, even if the site is closed. It should be kept in a binder or central repository so that the auditor and the foreman have quick and easy access. Other members of the project team will find these reports handy as well. The first thing an auditor should do is inventory the daily foreman's reports to ensure that they are all there. They should also ensure that all are signed. This will be source documentation for audit verification purposes. This report should be seen as a crucial and true communication of project progress.

Here is where the daily foreman's reports will come in handy:

1. Payroll testing – Match the number of people on payroll charged to the number of employees on-site per the report.
2. Holiday time – Verify that for holiday time the day fell on a holiday and this is reflected on the daily foreman report.
3. Weather/Work reconciliation – If site was closed early for weather, verify weather conditions against the report.
4. Claims verification – If an insurable loss has been reported, the facts can be verified or refuted by seeing what was included on the foreman report. This applies to both 'people claims' and 'property claims.' Property claims for weather can use the report to show no one was onsite or injured during the weather emergency. (You can not get hurt if you were not there.)
5. Change Order Auditing – A change order will spell out what is found. You can verify if these assumptions are correct by seeing what was mentioned in the daily foreman's report.
6. Equipment Testing – Since equipment is recorded and charged daily, part of the equipment invoice testing is to ensure the bill and the daily report reconcile.
7. Honesty of project manager – Many times when you ask a project manager how the project is going, they do not want to be an alarmist and they state things are fine. Many times, this is a rose-colored glass view with the hope that things will get better. An auditor should review the daily foreman's reports and assess whether they come to the same conclusion.

   A lot of vital information is recorded on a construction daily report, and it is important to have someone familiar with the project and always present at the site to consistently complete the form every day. If possible, it should be as simple as possible so that the report does not take up a lot of time. Most of it can be automated. A single person should be assigned the task of writing the report to make it consistent from day to day. Obviously if that person is not available for a particular day, it should be done by an assigned backup person. Upon return to the site, the foreman who usually does the report should review those from his absence. As part of the review, signing a signature or initial on the report is good, it proves that at least a cursory review was done.

The report can be used by the foreman as a reminder of what needs to be discussed during some of the many meetings he has to attend. The foreman delegates tasks to members of the construction team. The foreman can then note what was delegated to whom, creating a diary of the day's events. They may need to report to the union progress on apprentices' safety and training. The daily foreman's report is an excellent reference point to get the data that needs to be reported.

If the report can be automated, it will be easier to maintain consistency and completeness. This can be handy if claims or disputes arise. Automated reports may be easier to do, making the report less tedious to write. Additionally daily reports can be more accessible this way. Just be careful that if daily reports contain sensitive information, the access to it is limited.

Chapter 21

Perimeters and cameras

Perimeters on a construction site must be protected and inspected constantly. People by nature are curious and want to peek in on sites – especially little children. The exposure to debris, dust and sparks at a sight can badly injure a bystander.

REGULATORS

The law requires that construction sites are properly fenced to shield the public from noise pollution and possible injuries which could be sustained at the sites. Local jurisdictions will explain more on the requirements. Failure to meet these requirements can be seen as a criminal offense of neglect and can cause the local authorities to shut down the site or impose costly fines.

THEFT

Theft costs the construction industry about $1 billion annually.[1] Protecting the perimeter is important to reduce the risk of theft on the property. The item most stolen is anything containing copper. Also stolen are timber, metal, tools and equipment. Copper is usually found in cables and plumbing infrastructure. There has been a rise in theft of aluminum lately. Stealing from a construction site is illegal. To prosecute you need to determine who stole it.

Cameras are good for this, but you need to ensure that the videos are clear, timestamped and collectable. Having proper lights at the sight will deter people from entering the site to steal the copper and it will result in better pictures on the camera. Additional steps include, locking up copper when the site is unoccupied, fencing that cannot be cut (this is why you will see green tarp in front of a lot of fences), warning signs, enlisting the help of neighbors, painting copper leads black and proper perimeter monitoring. Whichever method the project teams opt for, the best solution is often a mix of solutions.

DOI: 10.1201/9781003461487-22

SABOTAGE

Sabotage happens. It happens often on construction projects and can be an inside job or an outside job. The usual suspects are an executive whose project was turned down, a disgruntled employee, employees afraid of making a change, a competitor, lobbyists or protest groups, or neighbors who do not want the project in their backyard. The more controversial the project is, the greater the risk of sabotage. For example, a new hospital will be at lower risk of sabotage than a nuclear plant. Saboteurs can become very creative to halt a construction or at least delay it. Some of the below is what has been seen over the years:

- 'Planting' artifacts at the site. Archaeological findings on the site are not unusual. When they are found they have to go through the following four phases:
  - Uncover them with little or no damage; also determine if there are more in the area.
  - Identify what they are.
  - Contact the authorities who will determine the safest way to remove them.
  - Decide what to do with them, which becomes more difficult if these findings are or possibly are unexploded weapons. Decisions include keeping them where they are and detouring around them, removing them and keeping them in a museum, or leaving them where they are and continuing construction anyway.
  - Removal of artifacts may be done but this is not a process that can be rushed or can be performed in all sorts of weather. It should not be done without the supervision of experts.

  In the case of historical findings, project progress will slow down as you need to call in the experts (archaeologists) who need to perform their own investigation, which involves manually removing soil around the area. This is a slow and tedious process. It is not simply digging the dirt of the ground. It is done with paintbrushes and picks so as not to disturb the artifacts. This alone will cause disruption to project progression.
- Planting endangered wildlife in the area. Wildlife may be animals or plants. If endangered wildlife is found, depending on what is planted, you may have to stop construction or postpone it until the wildlife is removed and safely transported elsewhere. In the case of nesting animals, it may require that the project come to a halt until the wildlife gives birth and the animals can be safely moved. Certain nesting birds may be protected and you will need to protect the nest.
- Squatters at the site. Squatters are people who enter an unused property and unlawfully occupy it. Removing them can be difficult and may involve the need to call law enforcement.

- One group sent e-mails and pamphlets to every employee who was going to move to their site and showed them the (inflated) crime statistics for the area.

PROTECTING CURIOUS BYSTANDERS

Construction sites are usually close to or in public spaces. They are often busy areas with many people passing by all day. But the site is dangerous, especially if you have never been on a site before. They have the potential to not only be damaged and vandalized, but they also pose the risk of harming others who enter them. Protecting the perimeter will help ensure that people know that it is a do-not-enter zone.

People are sometimes distracted and without perimeter protection they may enter the site and not even realize it. There may be no malice, just a lack of realization. Construction sites, especially when active, produce dust and other hazardous materials. Construction workers are protected with the safety equipment they use and respirators when necessary. General public walking by does not normally have that protection with them or in use. Keeping the perimeter safe and cordoned off will protect them from accidental inhalation of these particles. Face masks became popular after the Covid pandemic, but these face masks may not protect from the particles found in construction activity.

A locked door may be all you need as far as perimeter access. I remember one audit where there was a suite of offices being constructed. We were doing a walkthrough and one of the stops was a pediatrician. Suddenly, excited sounds came pouring out of the pediatric office. A child was missing. Knowing there was an office still being constructed I ran to that office to ensure the door was locked. It was not. With my heart pounding I surveyed the whole room and thankfully the child was not there. There were missing floorboards, an open ceiling, and many downed cables and lines. There were no workers there. I returned to the pediatrician's office and they found the child. He was asleep under the fish tank! It was a great relief but a valuable learning tool as well. We immediately took steps to have the door permanently locked.

FIRE PROTECTION

There are many flammable products on site and they all must be labeled. But it also needs to be protected from a carelessly thrown cigarette, being bumped into, moved into a high-traffic area or spilled.

In case a fire does breakout, there are four important pieces known as RACE:

1. Rescue
2. Alarm
3. Contain
4. Extinguish

Procedures should be in place to address all four components. Audit should review these procedures for completeness.

A construction site fire can cause significant damage not only to the construction site itself, but also to the workers within it and the public. This could result in significant injury to people while also destroying all progress that the site may have made. Having cameras on the site can allow monitoring to be done so that if a spark, smoke or a fire is detected, an alarm can be sounded and immediate action taken to douse out the fire.

There should be fire extinguishers nearby and accessible. I had one project where the fire extinguishers were posted at a height of about 8 feet. Many people would not be able to reach these quickly enough. Audit should see if the extinguishers are accessible and check the labels to ensure they are current and inspected.

The site should have clearly marked exit routes that are accessible. These routes may change weekly or monthly depending on construction progress. Marshals should be assigned to look for fire risks, fires and to evacuate when necessary. Fire marshals should be trained in how to extinguish fires, keeping in mind that some fires should not be put out with water. Sites should have alert systems in place to warn workers to evacuate. It is not as easy to evacuate a construction site as it is to evacuate an office. Office workers can just stop what they are doing and leave the building. Construction sites require that people stop what they are doing, put what they are doing in a neutral position, and then they can leave. Utilities may need to be turned off. Even looking for employees left behind can be more difficult.

To aid in evacuation, the site may also need to be equipped with boundary lighting. Activity involving open flames and fires should be ceased 1 hour before the end of the shift. Additional checks of hot sites should be performed every half an hour until there is no evidence of fire or smoldering fire. This will allow any hot spots to be returned to a safe state. These, however, are JUST guidelines. Hotter and dryer climates may require more time. Windy climates will require more time and more close supervision of hot spots.

NOTE

1 www.constructconnect.com/blog/five-steps-for-preventing-construction-site-theft

Chapter 22

Safety and safety equipment

Construction sites are not the safest place to walk by, stand in or be nearby. Auditors should visit the site (once prepared) but knowing where to focus your attention can be difficult. There are 10 basic areas of focus that an auditor should concentrate on:

1. Site review – conduct a full review of the site, both during work hours and after.
2. Equipment and machinery handling, including any indication of improper care.
3. Health and safety measures are in place at the site.
4. Documentation for all the health and safety such as evacuation rules, evacuation routes, first aid and any drills.
5. Communication and how communication is accessed on site.
6. Legal compliance and any records that need to be kept.
7. Proof of regular inspection and proof of any remedial action taken when inspections find issues.
8. Defects and repairs and how defects are reported and corrected.
9. Scaffolds and the erection of scaffolds by qualified individuals.
10. Ladders and the safe usage of ladders.

SITE REVIEW

Site review includes a walkthrough of the site, either announced or surprised, and the documentation. This should be a routine part of the job of the project manager and should be documented. If the project manager is not doing this, then the Safety Officer(s) should be doing it and documenting it. As I talk about in the Walkthrough and Inspections chapter, the auditor wants to go to the site and ensure, at least from a common-sense perspective, that employees are being safe. Things to look for include, using two small ladders instead of one large one, using safety goggles when using anything that creates sparks or dust, not using harnesses to work at significant heights

DOI: 10.1201/9781003461487-23

(over 6 feet off the ground), not paying attention when using welding guns or circular saws, and look at how others are kept away from hazardous equipment (they should not be chatting with another worker while leaning on a chipper shredder). Audit should note any workers that appear to be fooling around or not taking safety seriously. Any person who appears physically or mentally impaired should be asked to leave the site.

Once while walking a site, a senior auditor was with me. The senior auditor had recently undergone surgery. He was using a cane for balance but was otherwise feeling well. I questioned if he should come but he stated he was fine. Upon checking in at the front desk to enter the site, they would not let him on site. He explained that he was the auditor but was still refused access. The auditor was not happy but returned to the office and I carried on with the walkthrough. In this case, the front desk was correct. Even though he was not a worker, it was not safe for him to walk the site.

On another occasion, we were walking a site and found two workers in the back of two cherry pickers. They were waiting for the driver and were going to be clearing a tree on the power lines. The boom of the cherry picker was already extended. Bored of waiting for the driver, the two started fooling around and were sword fighting with long shears between the two cherry pickers. Despite wearing harnesses, neither man had them tethered. The driver arrived and drove them a few feet to the site. They were clearing trees near electric lines. Audit found several issues with this:

1. Harnesses were not tethered.
2. Unsafe use of long shears.
3. The cherry picker should not be extended until in place.
4. Workers were horse-playing.
5. Workers should not be in the boom unless there are other workers acting as spotters.
6. Cherry pickers should not be driven while someone is in the boom.
7. Work near active utility lines should be done or supervised by the utility company.

EQUIPMENT AND MACHINERY HANDLING

Equipment should only be operated by those trained to do so. There are special considerations to ensure safe usage. It is therefore important that not just anyone operates the machinery. They need to be trained professionals!

Communication may be a factor. When you are in a crane or a bulldozer, it can be difficult to hear, and the operator should be wearing ear protection. For this reason, there should be a set of hand signals that is used by a designated signal person. The signal person is a second set of eyes for the operator and knows the operator's blind spots. Working together will create a safer environment.

If equipment is not being used on a solid base, it is at risk of turning over. Part of the way to protect this is rollover protection structures, such as cages, that protect the driver in case of emergency. Just like a motor vehicle, the driver should be using a seatbelt. In the case of a rollover, this will help prevent him from flying off the machine. Many times, when watching sites, if a bulldozer or other equipment needs to be moved, you see an operator just jump in and move it. This is not safe. It takes longer to access the machinery correctly but its importance should not be taken lightly.

Equipment should be inspected to ensure that they are in working condition. This would be maintenance as recommended by the manufacturer. Audit should collect checklists that show the machinery was inspected and repaired when necessary. Operators should check the equipment daily – mostly the braking system and steering system. Any problems should result in immediate remediation.

Equipment inventory should be done on a daily basis to ensure nothing is missing. We touch on this in other areas of the book, parking equipment in unique shapes is an easy way to quickly see if anything is missing. This check should be done before the shifts start, if not, the person will need to waste a lot of time finding equipment on the site.

Currently on the news, they are talking about a 12-year-old boy who stole a forklift and took it on a joy ride. The forklift was left on an open site. The boy was able to get into the forklift and found the keys which were hidden in the forklift. Luckily no one was hurt but he did damage several vehicles in the process. So, who is to blame; the boy or whoever did not properly lockup the forklift?[1]

Equipment accidents are usually severe and, in many cases, fatal. It is critical to ensure guidelines are followed to protect the operators and others on the site.

HEALTH AND SAFETY MEASURES IN PLACE AT THE SITE

Many times, in construction, health and safety involves what to do in case of emergency. Of course, we want the workers to always be careful and think about safety first, but accidents do happen. The biggest battle, sometimes, is setting the mentality. How do you get workers to think about safeguarding. Requiring the use of Personal Protective Equipment (PPE) helps set the tone. PPE includes shoes, hardhat, high-visibility clothing, protective eye wear, face masks and gloves. Depending on the job being done there may be more. Having extra on hand is recommended.

Safety as an attitude is something cheap and easy that project management can control. Safety should be discussed at all meetings, reiterated with continuing education and with safety propaganda, such as posters around the site. Hydration should be encouraged, especially in hot and humid climates. Hydration stations should be established and used. Motivate and reward safety. Anything that can make people remember that the importance of the day is that they go home each night, safely.

DOCUMENTATION FOR ALL THE HEALTH AND SAFETY SUCH AS EVACUATION RULES, EVACUATION ROUTES, FIRST AID AND ANY DRILLS

It is human nature that in an emergency you call 911 and first aid responds. On construction sites this may not be the best practice. Safety officers are medically trained and being on the site can more quickly respond to an emergency and stabilize an injured person while waiting for 911 to respond. Therefore, it must be required that in order to do any work on the site, a safety officer must be on site.

Evacuation routes need to be clearly marked so that workers can evacuate safely while avoiding any danger zones. This is hard as sometimes the whole evacuation route can change as work progresses. Think about it. If there is an empty space in the morning that incorporates at area that gets trenched in the afternoon, problems can result during evacuation.

COMMUNICATION AND HOW COMMUNICATION IS ACCESSED ON SITE

Construction can be an indoor or outdoor activity. A worker won't know what infrastructure is around until he gets there. Chances are there will not be a phone line or if there is it may be limited and primitive. Granted we all rely on cell phones nowadays, but there is also no assurance that the worker is in cell range nor requirements that limit or forbid phones on site. Chances are there are walkie talkie systems at least for supervision. In case of emergency, where communication is needed there needs to be a communication plan in place. There should be a communication plan for the project as well. I encourage auditors to obtain a copy. Be careful many responsibilities or numbers may be listed as 'TBD' or to be determined. Audit should ensure that TBD is replaced with a real person or phone number quickly.

LEGAL COMPLIANCE AND ANY RECORDS THAT NEED TO BE KEPT

Compliance with local and organizational procedures should be addressed in the project manual or as part of the contract. Audit should find out from the local board what records need to be kept. Audit should subsequentially ensure that those documents are being maintained and that they are safe.

PROOF OF REGULAR INSPECTION AND PROOF OF ANY REMEDIAL ACTION TAKEN WHEN INSPECTIONS FIND ISSUES

Inspections need to be done and they may be carried out by various different people. Local zoning or building departments may have different requirements for these inspections. Again, audit should check with the local government as to the result of these inspections. Before moving in to the facility, local inspections have to be done. Audit should ensure that there were no issues with the inspection.

There are trends where inspectors are receiving bribes to pass properties. Audit wants to ensure that there are no expenses coming through for facilitation payments – this may be indicative of a bribe.

DEFECTS AND REPAIRS AND HOW DEFECTS ARE REPORTED AND CORRECTED

When defects are noted with working conditions, equipment or temporary facilities on site, what procedures must be followed? What number should it be reported to? Who ensures that defects are fixed efficiently and thoroughly?

SCAFFOLDS AND THE ERECTION OF SCAFFOLDS BY QUALIFIED INDIVIDUALS

Scaffolds need to be erected on solid level ground and must be done by a qualified person. There is no specific licensing or qualifications, but OSHA lays out some standards such as building, erection, dismantling, moving, operation, repair, maintenance or inspection. These standards are to protect the scaffold and employees from falls, falling objects, structural instability and overloading. It also established standards to prevent electrocution. OSHA has established responsibility for standards to state and local government. These conditions must, at a minimum, meet OSHA standards. Most of the requirements for the standard are very technical and outside the scope of a normal audit, but the auditor can still discuss with the project manager if the scaffold was erected safely and has anyone been injured due to scaffold instability. If there have been incidences, Audit should collect details about the incident(s) to see if there is any pattern emerging. Audit can also add value by testing that workers have been trained in scaffold safety. It is best to get this proof from the vendor each worker is with. Failing that, workers will need to be interviewed and asked if they have been trained. While on the scaffold, workers should be tethered, specifics about this would be detailed in the local code.

LADDERS AND THE SAFE USAGE OF LADDERS

There are three important rules when using ladders. The first is to use the right ladder for the job. You should not be stacking ladders to get high enough, use the correct ladder.

The second is you should always have three contact points on the ladder at all times. The three contact points are two legs and an arm. You can have one arm off to do whichever task you are doing, but you should not be leaning over too far to do it.

Number three, tether up. Any ladder work should be done with at least one spotter and with the worker tethered in. When looking at ladder work, no employee should be alone. The risk of falls is high, no matter how used to it you are.

As you can see there is a lot to be considered about maintaining a safe working environment for laborers, neighbors, vendors, suppliers and anyone else who comes near the site. Before doing the site visit, Audit should do the background of obtaining copies of plans, communication protocols, emergency responses and drills before they even step out onto the site. When performing a walkthrough or inspection, audit should rely on checklists to ensure that are testing everything necessary. Additionally, inspections should not be a one-off thing. It should be done on different dates to ensure consistency. It should also be done as unannounced as possible.

NOTE

1 Fox News, November 28, 2023, Michigan Boy Steals Forklift from Middle School, leads police on chase.

Chapter 23

Budgets and budget reporting

Maintaining budgets and sticking to budgets is a good way to keep control over your construction projects. Most people when they hear budget assume I am talking about money. This is not a valid assumption. When talking about project management, there are budgets for time and/or budgets for money. Budgeting for a project is not easy, especially as there are so many minute moving parts. I like to think of budgeting like a Lego set.

The original timeline and the original budget should be fixed as baselines and progress from there should be measured against the baseline. Budget for change orders, or contingency, should be kept as well but it should be clear on the budget that it is for contingency. Many will try to combine the two, and this should not be done; it is better for data analysis if these figures are segregated. In other words, contingency is its own Lego structure.

When it comes to budget or cost there are four approaches to determine what is needed:

TOP-DOWN APPROACH

The top-down approach is when the budget is started by taking the funds approved by the investment committee and then breaking it down to the smaller buckets of project detail. When making decisions during the project, the project manager will use the budgeted amount to help make the decision. The decision to allocate the funds into the smaller buckets considers past experience and current market conditions. In this case, the Lego pieces are dumped on the center of the table and you can divide it into all the little pieces and then just BUILD!

BOTTOM-UP APPROACH

The bottom-up approach is when the budget is created by adding up all the different line items and estimates of material and supplies as laid out by the architects. There are people in the industry who can determine costs

DOI: 10.1201/9781003461487-24

for projects and estimate needs. This method often results in more accurate estimates. In this case, I have broken the project down into small pieces and I know exactly which Lego bricks I need. All I have to do is collect them and build them. I may grab a few extras, just in case.

PARAMETRIC

Parametric estimating is based on historical data but breaks the project down into units. For example, if you were doing an apartment building renovation and you know each apartment takes 200 hours and $30,000 to renovate, you would know that for 1000 apartments, it will take 200,000 hours and $30,000,000. What this does not consider is the learning curve and economies of scale. We mentioned the learning curve before, but to reiterate, it is the fact that tasks get faster and faster solely out of repetition. With economies of scale, you can group parts for multiple apartments together and save money and you can do some things in bulk or as a common area, completing work quicker. With our Legos, it is sometimes easier to work on common areas of a frame and build in customization to form a cohesive unit.

ANALOGOUS

The last way is through analogous budgeting. Though a tricky word to say and spell, it is simply benchmarking. The project spend and time are based on other projects of a similar nature with slight adjustments in certain areas. In this case, when you build your Lego structure, you know how many pieces it takes already and you know how long it takes to construct.

The method used for estimating is irrelevant to Audit, as this is the decision of the project manager. For all intents and purposes, the project manager has probably used a combination of the four methods to allocate the cost and time. The concern of audit is how much the project deviates from what was planned, and if possible, why did these deviations occur.

A budget is the total project costs for the costs broken down into small components and scheduling disbursements over the various phases. Creating the project is an integral function of project management. The budgets for your project are like a gas gauge. It tells you how much you have left to spend as you navigate through the project. Not only will the project manager use it to make decisions, but the budget can also be shared with others to let them know how everything is progressing.

Having a budget allows the project manager to:

1. Set goals for spending
2. Figure out categories that he can borrow from to keep the project on track

3. Find hidden savings via economies of scale
4. Modify plans to make better financial decisions
5. Reduce stress

By setting goals, the project manager will be better prepared to understand where the project stands without or before doing earned value management. If he knows that something is about to happen, he can better predict the financial impact of the event and possibly minimize the impact. Let's say the cost of steel is increasing. This is a major cost to the project and the project manager wants to see what alternatives he has. He may decide instead of using Russian steel, if they switch to Brazilian steel, it may be less of an impact on the budget.

Just like we expect the architect to value engineer the design during the planning phase, continuing the exercise throughout the project can also provide fruitful results. This can be done sometimes, not by changing the goods used but by ordering goods in bigger batches, spreading the needs out against multiple vendors or taking advantage of other opportunities.

The more the budget is broken down the easier it is to analyze. You may have one vendor who is going over budget, but the rest of the project is running smoothly so it is hard to tell that things are awry. Fortunately, you can monitor the cost budget quite easily. When invoices come in, they are generally accompanied by a schedule of value that shows the amount budgeted and the amount completed to date (Figure 23.1).

Be careful, however, as the scheduled value may show change orders that have been approved. It is important for the auditor to know if change orders were included. If they have, the auditor now has a testing advantage. When testing change orders, they can ensure that they have received the full population if they can see that the scheduled value – collected change orders – revert back to the original budget (which will be on the schedule of value for Invoice 1).

I have already pointed out several times, time is sometimes more important than cost in the project success priority. In many instances we have time budgets, though that is not what we call them. These are better known as milestones or time frames. The only difference is that instead of accounting for every cent, the time budget can account for every second.

Once the budget is established, managing to budget is the important part. This can be done in six steps:

1. Create the outline and timeline. In order to do this project must be broken into detailed 'chunks.'
2. Compile all identified costs into a comprehensive, overall project budget.
3. Look at ways to save money and maximize efficiency.
4. As savings are identified, flag any additional budget pieces.
5. Research relevant market prices before finalizing any purchases or contracts with vendors.
6. Constantly look for alternatives.

Schedule of Values

Project Name:
Project #:
Contractor:

Application #:
Application Date:
Period to:

Item #	Description of Work	Scheduled Value	WORK COMPLETED		Stored Materials (not in Work Completed)	Total Completed Stored to Date	% Complete	Balance to Finish	Retainage*
			Previous Application	This Period					10%
9970	Demolition	$ 3,000.00	$ 2,000.00	$ -	$ -	$ 2,000.00	67%	$ 1,000.00	$ 200.00
9955	Drywall & Carpentry	$ 36,000.00	$ 11,000.00	$ 4,200.00	$ 1,800.00	$ 17,000.00	47%	$ 19,000.00	$ 1,700.00
9940	Doors & Hardware	$ 1,000.00	$ -	$ 500.00	$ -	$ 500.00	50%	$ 500.00	$ 50.00
9943	Electrical	$ 7,000.00	$ 1,000.00	$ 3,000.00	$ 850.00	$ 4,850.00	69%	$ 2,150.00	$ 485.00
Totals		$ 47,000.00	$ 14,000.00	$ 7,700.00	$ 2,650.00	$ 24,350.00	52%	$ 22,650.00	$ 2,435.00

Figure 23.1 Sample Schedule of Value.

What needs to happen is that open communications are encouraged. When the project manager identifies savings, they should share this with the team – up to management and down through the supply chain. Often, they do not, they just earmark it in case it is needed later. Auditors can ask directly if savings were found and encourage congratulations and kudos when this happens.

CASE STUDY

The Audit team for a franchise company decided to start implementing construction audits. The goal was to look at some of the franchise locations that were constructed and repaid by the parent company. Since construction audit was never done before it was unclear which franchise to start with. It was decided to start with the branch most over budget. Audit ran some data analytic tests using this criterion and it turned out that projects were never over budget.

This either means there was something wrong with the data, the process or the funding of the branches. Audit started with the data, thinking that was easiest. The data was looked at manually to ensure it was not a script error and sure enough all branches came in under budget. Audit then decided to pull the funding sheets to ensure that there was no problem with the data. They pulled 15 sites and in 12 of them, the funding sheets were less than what it said on the data sheet. It was not clear what was happening and Audit decided to do an operational audit to see if they could find the problem.

They walked through the process with one of the project managers. The audit started with location. Sites were evaluated for competition, traffic in the area and proximity to other branches. Information was given to the franchise department which would approve the location and apply funding based on investment committee and franchisee contracts. A test of 20 locations found nothing outside the norm.

Audit proceeded to the next step which was the assignment of project management. The process followed that project managers were divided into geographical regions and there were two to five project managers depending on the location. The secretary divided the properties up by distributing folders that were identified by a location number and files were sealed as confidential. The secretary only knew who got each number, they did not know any more specifics about who got what. It was explained that this process was put in place as many project managers were fighting for certain locations and there were accusations of favoritism in assignments. Audit found no issues with this process and was able to look at a report which showed an even distribution of properties per property manager.

Next the project manager would set it up in the system. They would input all the demographics from the file and the amount budgeted for the work. This is where the process fell short. Audit asked the facilities area to walk them through the system. The system was accessible via a terminal in the facility office. There was a general login in use. The administrator came in each morning and signed onto the system. The system could be used by anyone in the office. It was explained that allowed the vendors and contractors to go on so they could access documents that were cloud-based and to check e-mails or do Google searches. Generally, they were only on the system for 10 minutes or so. The administrator explained that it made her job easier, as they no longer were 'borrowing' her computer. Audit decided to investigate this system.

On the desktop there was a folder labeled budgets. Audit opened the documents and found all the projects out there and the budget. Audit questioned the administrator. It was explained that after funding was approved, they placed the budget in this folder. This made it so much easier when someone needed to reference one of the budgets as they were there for all to see. Audit found out how they were so 'efficient.' If a project went over budget, they simply added funds to the budget amount in the folder. There was no audit trail as it was always issued from the same 'general' computer. There was no way to know if the budgets were changed by the project manager or the contractor. When the project was completed, they used the information in the budgets folder to close the project.

Chapter 24

Month-end reporting

Managing a project is tough work. With lots of tasks to oversee, it can be daunting to keep up and provide updates on project status. It can be helpful or harmful to focus the project manager's attention as to what needs to be done. To provide the right information and to maintain proper focus, a project manager can benefit from producing a monthly status report.

A project management report is a document that provides information on the project's progress, performance and overall status. It serves as a key instrument for projects of all types and is used by key stakeholders, including:

- Project sponsors
- Top-level executives
- Project managers
- Team members

The report visualizes your project's realities and performance during the month. It acts as a conversation point for project managers and executives to compare progress to plan and talk about what needs the project has going forward. It is important to have this conversation, as many times the executives can help move barriers or get departments to help when a roadblock is met.

Month-end reporting is an important tool in the project management process but it is often overlooked. A month-end report does not need to be too detailed or too formal but should address certain items, some of which can be carried over from the prior months' reports. It should include:

- Project name and project code
- Amount spent to date
- Budget at completion
- Change orders to date
- Anticipated scope of work for the month (this can be taken from last month's report)
- What was actually accomplished in the month

DOI: 10.1201/9781003461487-25

- Safety incidents
- Days where site was closed (planned and unplanned)
- Change orders for the month and allocation of change order costs (owner, contractor, or architect)
- New emerging risks and contingencies (if available)
- Work planned for next month
- Any issues that may prevent progress and contingencies
- Earned Value Management figures
- Graphs to support budget and change orders
- Status of key KPIS

Some of this information is already available. Remember the daily foreman's reports?

Graphs are recommended for these reports as data is being sent up to executives who are distant from the project. The monthly report may be given as a quick review of the project. Before making a chart it's important to understand why you need one. Charts, maps and infographics help people understand complicated data, find patterns, identify trends and tell a story. Think about the message you want to share with your audience. But keep it simple (Figure 24.1).

Follow best charting practices. Your numbers need to add up and charts need to be scaled accordingly. What would you like to show? Being open and honest in these charts will lead to executives having fewer questions and will leave the project manager available to manage the project. Having an

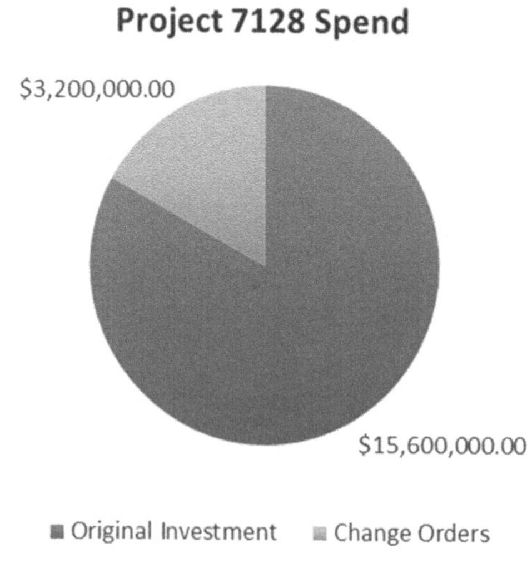

Figure 24.1 Example of effective charting for month-end reporting.

initial conversation with management about what is important to them and how they would like it presented can be valuable.

Many times, status reports are afraid to mention lags or negative news as they feel they can make up for it later. The auditor should stay on the lookout for this. When deciding what chart to use, keep in mind the readability of some charts. Many people can read a pie chart or bar graph but if you start adding cone charts or radar charts then you may be losing the point of using a chart. It is a chance to tell stakeholders the project story, not the knowledge the project manager has in charting.

A good project manager will take the report writing process as an opportunity to look back on the project and assess how accurate their estimates were, this can come in handy for the future. Reports should focus on baselines originally created and compare them to actual ones, again using this as a learning tool for future projects. It gives the project manager a chance to possibly see emerging trends and then use those trends as an advantage or a change to rectify negative trends or bottlenecks before they get out of hand. There is normally a monthly construction meeting on projects. Using the monthly report, the project manager can attend this meeting with a solid agenda and know what the meeting needs to focus on and prioritize.

CASE STUDY

I was working on an audit where the project manager told us the project was going 'so smoothly it didn't even need to be audited.' He relayed the same information to executive management. This was a sign that audit was most definitely needed. He had given a presentation for the board of project status, and it was very scarce. It was two or three bullets long and said: Cost to date $6,000,000, Incidents to date 0, Status of schedule – ahead. He said everything was fine and he could not ask for better results. The board gave us (audit) one month to agree or disagree with the project manager. We did some testing and ran the numbers.

- Safety concerns were popping up, they went from three incidences a week to seven! Several employees required medical attention. When we asked the project manager why no incidents were noted, the response was: 'no one has died, yet.' Two employees were put on short-term disability. These incidents happened before the board presentation. The causes of the accidents were all avoidable and were due to employees tripping over trenches. All were driven to the local emergency room; safety officers were on duty but not reachable.
- Cameras on-site were empty and not recording. Audit was able to see that the cameras were there but when they asked for the tapes, none were available. Audit asked to see where the cameras were being monitored from. They were not.

- Two vendors were clashing often to the point where it was affecting project progress. They were fighting over how to do work and who was able to have access to materials.
- A review of payroll showed that 35 of 50 laborers were being overpaid. We were told a project at the end would be done to fix this.
- Several employees had no social security numbers.
- Invoices were mathematically inaccurate.
- Change orders could not be reviewed as the project manager did not have them sorted in any way, they were all just thrown in a box. Due to the one-month timeline, we shelved this object as it would take considerable time to get this sorted.
- Payments made showed the project was financially 75% of the GMAX used; this was concerning as the construction was still in the early stages – only the shell had been constructed.

By the end of the month, we concluded that the rosy picture painted by the project manager was inaccurate. We put policies in place to require month-end reporting and the information needed was templated. The project manager was not allowed to leave blanks. We also automated the report so that Earned Value Management formulas were completed and charted. If certain variances at completion levels were hit, a memo was automatically sent to Treasury Management. Lastly, we were able to input all the change orders and sort them effectively. We found that at least 1/3 of the change orders that were approved should not have been.

Chapter 25

Walkthroughs and inspection

As I mentioned earlier, before an auditor enters a site, they should be trained on-site safety. Keeping in mind that the site is unsafe, I would recommend that the walkthrough team be limited and everyone on the team is not impaired in any way that can make a walkthrough a risk. The people on the walkthrough should be wearing proper footwear and hard hats. If the team does not have hard hats, it may be possible to get them from the sign-in desk, along with a hi-vis vest.

Walkthroughs should be done at every phase of the construction process. I encourage the auditor to bring a checklist with them to document any findings. The checklist should include:

- Project name
- Date of walkthrough
- Number/name of people on walkthrough
- Time of walkthrough
- Weather conditions
- Number of employees on-site that day or a copy of the sign-in sheet
- Photos of any violations. Cell phone photos should suffice and be encouraged as they are easy to carry and will apply a date stamp to all photos. Ask permission to use a phone on-site before you take photos. Do not use flash.

Though the auditor is not an OSHA expert there are certain items that are common sense and should be noted.

- The site was secured and to do a walkthrough you had to pass a guard or have a door unlocked for you.
- Workers not speaking English or the native language.
- Workers working alone even though they are doing ladder work.
- Unsafe ladder usage (using the wrong tool for the job). Safe ladder usage should mean the worker is touching the ladder with at least three parts of the body and not overly stretching.

DOI: 10.1201/9781003461487-26

- Workers without proper shoes, safety goggles, vest and/or hard hat. Note any workers who have duct tape used on their shoes or to keep their smock on.
- Workers doing anything greater than 6 feet without harness.
- Workers with obvious wounds.
- Workers involved in horse play.
- Workers appearing to operate machinery without care.
- Workers smoking while working or near flammable goods.
- Workers using cell phones while working.
- Stairwells without handrails and no fall warning signs.
- Stairwells that are incomplete but not cordoned off.
- Workers carrying bulky items without the assistance of a spotter.
- Idle workers.
- Signs of alcohol or drug use (empty bottles).
- Trash and food waste on-site; signs of rat, mice or other infestations.
- A messy site that can be an additional trip hazard.
- Workers working alone (there should also be at least two people on-site in case of accident or emergency.
- Excess water pooling.
- Workers not wearing headphones in areas of high machine volume.

Walkthroughs out of hours are recommended to ensure that no one can access the site, there is no equipment or material lying around and security asks why they are there (hopefully security is present). I do not recommend that an auditor go to the site without letting anyone know but it should still be on a need-to-know basis – the head of security should definitely be one to be notified. I would stress to the head of security to keep the visit as confidential as possible.

If a site is using cameras, the auditor should sample a few days' worth of tapes and verify that the tapes are usable, have a clear package and appear not to be damaged or tampered with. The auditor can then do a visual walkthrough using the same checklist as above, but the checklist should be clearly noted that this was just a visual walkthough and not a live one. Lastly an inventory of tapes should be done. An auditor will want to ensure that if tapes are reused, the prior footage is backed up to an accessible location. This should be done in case of insurance claims.

At the end of the project a walkthrough should also be done, before the release of final retainage. It is usually done by one or two members of the project team and the contractor. I recommend that audit attends the final walkthrough, if invited. This final walkthrough takes users or project members through the final project. The walkthrough is a final inspection of the project and the creation of what we call a punch list. A punch list is a list of items that still need to be done to leave the property in perfect condition.

This may include small cosmetic items, such as paint runs, carpets not quite squared, missing furniture, etc. There is generally money withheld for them to fix these items and final retainage should not be released until these items are cleared. The amount to be withheld is specified (or should be specified) in the contract.

Chapter 26

Insurance

As auditors we know the five strategies of risk are: assume and accept, avoid, mitigate, transfer and monitor. Throughout this book, I talked about auditing and control steps that satisfy the mitigate aspect. Acceptance would be to do nothing and accept risks as part of doing business. But how do we transfer risk? Some of it can be transferred through the use of contracts as we discussed in the contract sessions. But there is another transfer strategy as well – insurance.

Besides protecting the owner, there are types of insurance to ensure that the contractor or subcontractor will remain solvent if something goes wrong on the project. After all, protecting them ensures that they can stay on the project until project completion.

VALIDATING THE INSURANCE

When auditing insurance, many auditors collect the certificate of insurance, which is acceptable, but I would recommend calling the company as well. This will give the auditor a better sense of insurance validity.

A certificate of insurance tells you:

- The name and address of the insured
- Policy number
- Coverage period
- Additional Insured
- Identification and location of the property being insured
- Insurer's name and contact information
- Types of coverage provided and their limits
- Policy deductibles
- Premiums charged (including discounts, if any)
- Endorsements or riders to the policy
- Claims reporting (optional) and broker/agent contacts.

DOI: 10.1201/9781003461487-27

An owner would ask to be an additional insured to help protect the property or project. This means that in the case of an insurable loss, the owner and the contractor would both be named on any checks or payouts. As additional insured, the owner would be notified of any cancellations of the policy. It is an additional control that I highly recommend to my clients. It does not increase the premiums. If the owner is not listed as additional insured nor does the contract specify that the owner should be an additional insured, a discussion with risk management should follow.

If auditing a fixed fee or design-build contract, insurance is non-tangible (only seen if a claim comes up) – it should be verified. Many times, we see that if projects are running out of money the insurance gets dropped. This is a risky move and if the owner is not asking for the policy, the only way it would be caught is if an insurable loss occurs. Some contractors decide to take the risk.

TYPES OF INSURANCE

There are various different types of insurance to consider on the project. For details as to what is covered and what is not, the auditor will need to reference the insurance policy or call the insurance company. The below list contains the most common types of insurance. Though some seem like they protect the contractor more than the property, you would be right. But if you go back to what we discussed during key stakeholders, the general contractor is a stakeholder where, if they fail, it could be disastrous.

- Builder's risk. Builder's risk insurance covers buildings that are under the course of construction but not yet completed. This insurance is good for new buildings as well as renovations to existing buildings. Normally this insurance will cover foundation work, equipment on site, nearby buildings and structures, temporary structures such as scaffolding cages, perimeter fencing whether it is permanent or fixed, and landscape features added by the builder. The insurance covers anything from losses due to fire, weather, vandalism or theft. This insurance is also called course of construction insurance.
- Product liability. Product liability is a special type of insurance that protects the cost of compensating anyone who gets injured by faulty construction that the contractor designs or supplies. Let's say a user moves on Day 1 and gets electrocuted because the outlet was not grounded, that might be covered. Due to the construction of support beams, you want to ensure that the scaffold contractor has product liability as well as the contractor. Product liability compensates for personal injury, loss or damage to property as a result of faulty construction and other unforeseen issues that could not be identified earlier. Due to exclusions, it may not cover faulty products resulting from bad

workmanship or financial loss to a person or business. Organizations can be held liable for faulty products even if they do not manufacture them. This would include equipment or material used in the course of construction.

- Employee dishonesty. Employee dishonesty is a type of crime insurance. This is particularly important to have in place if the construction workers will be interacting with the public. It can help you recover inventory and revenue that was lost due to employee dishonesty. Dishonesty includes:
  - Theft
  - Burglary
  - Embezzlement
  - Forgery
  - Credit card fraud
  - Check tampering
  - Fake invoices and receipts (usually found with travel and expense fraud).

  In some areas employee dishonesty is also known as discovery coverage or loss sustained coverage. The difference with loss sustained coverage is that you are covered during the period that the project is ongoing with the possibility of continued coverage for up to a year. Discovery coverage is usually good for claims, regardless of when they are discovered.
- Automobile or commercial vehicle insurance. Automobile coverage will generally be cheaper than commercial vehicle insurance, but be careful. It is cheaper is because automobile insurance will not cover all commercial vehicles. Commercial vehicles are vehicles used for business purposes. It generally covers accidents, theft and damage. It should cover both company-owned and leased vehicles. Some policies will include in the commercial vehicle coverage personal injury cover, goods in transit coverage, etc. It is possible that the contractor may have Motor Fleet insurance which is a bulk policy for all vehicles owned by the contractor, regardless of driver.
- Property. Property insurance is a broad term that applies to a policy or policies that provide property protection coverage or liability coverage for property owners. It covers any damage due to floods (maybe – it depends on the policy), weather, theft, earthquake, fire, vandalism, etc. It covers any individual other than the property owner who is injured on the property and may decide to file a lawsuit.
- Completed operations insurance. Completed operations insurance is a special policy that covers a contractor's liability for property damage or injuries to a third party once construction ceases. It can cover breach of contract damage or negligence claims. In such a case, the insurance company provides legal protection and defense and pays for any settlement that follows.

- Errors and omissions. Errors and omissions policy or E&O covers professional services. It protects organizations against errors, mistakes or oversights incurred during the project. This includes missing deadlines, failure to exercise due care and breach of contract. It also covers damages from wrongdoing to others. It normally does not cover errors and omissions done intentionally in furtherance of fraud or crime.
- Umbrella policy. I like to call an umbrella policy an 'if all else fails' policy. It covers for events that are not covered under any of the above policies.

Deciding which policies are needed is the role of risk management and the organization's project representative. This may already be set by policy.

Popular in construction projects are OCIP and CCIP policies. If you come across these terms, here's what it means. OCIP policies are Owner Controlled Insurance Policies that are owned by a property owner during construction or renovation. It is designed to cover all liability and loss of traditional policies in a single policy. They may be called wrap-up policies. In the case of OCIPs, the contractors and subcontractors are listed as additional insured.

Generally when these exist, the owner should be getting credit on invoices for the project's portion of policy costs. Auditor should ensure that the credit is being applied and is for the correct amount. Companies that routinely do construction as part of business (such as airports) would generally use OCIP policies.

The benefit of using an OCIP policy is there is a reduced risk of the insurance lapsing without the owner knowing about it.

A CCIP policy is a Contractor Controlled Insurance Policy. It is an insurance program that is controlled and managed by the project manager, construction manager or general contractor. It covers all the insurance for contractors and subcontractors and helps ensure that sufficient coverage is in place for most events that may happen. It generally does not extend to vendors and suppliers. Using CCIP is done to help save costs. In order to compensate for the insurance, there will generally be a deduction in the contract prices to reflect the cost of the CCIP.

Chapter 27

Labor and professional fees

There are three main components of all costs of construction: labor, material and equipment. According to the Construction Labor Market Analyzer, labor accounts for 20%–40% of the total construction costs.[1] Labor charges are not just wages, they include payroll taxes, time off, insurance, training, recruitment and other components. When auditing labor we call these components the labor burden. It is generally a multiplier of the salary or an agreed upon (contracted) amount that was negotiated in advance. The agreed-upon amounts are generally by title and not by employee.

The way labor burden is calculated should be spelled out in the contract but Audit should look at the calculation to ensure it is correct. It may also include union dues. Labor burden may include unemployment insurance. This is fine. However, if you have a CCIP policy (see previous chapter) ensure that it does not also include unemployment insurance. If not, you have two bites taken out of the same apple.

SAMPLE AUDIT PLAN FOR LABOR BURDEN

1. Identify the clause in the contract that specifies labor burden.
2. List out all amounts for each component.
3. Review the clause in the contract about general conditions.
4. Ensure that no items in general conditions overlap with labor burden.
5. Verify component figures with the vendor's Human Resources department or with the union board.
6. Recalculate rates used for accuracy.

AUDITING OVERTIME

The calculation for overtime is [(Hours worked – 40) * (agreed hourly rate) * 1.5)]. When applying labor burden to these figures, not all components are includable (time off, training days) as these do not change if the worker

DOI: 10.1201/9781003461487-28

works over 40 hours. Additionally, overtime is only paid to workers who get an hourly rate. Foremen and managers do not get overtime. Lastly, ensure that the first 40 hours are all worked on the same project.

HUMAN TRAFFICKING

There has been an uptick in human trafficking cases, especially in construction. In the aspect of human trafficking, everyone can play a role. A worker or auditor performing a walkthrough of a construction site should look out for clues. Suspicions should be addressed with Senior Management, Human Resources and if necessary, law enforcement. This should be done right away, do not wait until the report goes out. It is important to be vigilant and even open to a person seeking help. This opportunity can be their best chance of being saved. Some things to look out for include:

- Injured workers whose injuries appear old or who show signs of multiple bruises and scars.
- Workers who appear overly introverted or scared. They may show no eye contact even when approached. They may also flinch a lot as if they are afraid of being harmed.
- Inability to speak up for themselves, even when questioned.
- No identification is being carried by them.
- They do not know their social security number nor have any other government ID.
- A person who is unaware of their surroundings or location.
- Workers who appear unwashed or unhygienic.
- Workers with ill-fitting clothing and footwear.

Look for patterns, such as workers who do not speak English or do not appear to know what they are doing. Other signs are workers who appear unwell or sick, yet they continue to show up every day; they may have chronic coughs or skin infections.

As part of the costs associated with labor, it is difficult to pinpoint how many hours it will take to get the job done. So many factors can impact the number of hours – skill set of the workers, cohesiveness of the team, weather, health of the workers, room to work, etc. Even with a productive team, their productivity may be hindered by reliance on dependencies (items that need to get done first before they can proceed).

Generally, for safety purposes, work should be done in a well-lit area, so having adequate lighting needs to be a priority. Failure to have light may mean that the site needs to operate on curfew. Even if workers are using a stand light partnered with perimeter lighting, some tasks may be too risky to do once it is dark.

Certain localities will have curfew requirements that state all noise and construction must stop at a given time. If this is the case, the auditor should find out what that time is and anyone working 15 minutes past that time should have time denied. Anything past this should have already been denied by the project manager, anyway. Allowing 15 minutes enables the worker to clean up their station and leave the site.

REGULATIONS

There are regulations about minimum and maximum ages that can work on-site. In the USA, each worker must be more than 16, but they are limited to the number of hours they are allowed to work, as well as the type of tasks they can do. This is according to the Fair Labor Standards Act. There may be additional restrictions under local laws.

INSPECTION SCHEDULING

Certain tasks must be halted when inspections are due. It is therefore important that if inspections are due or coming close to being due, the project manager notifies the inspecting bodies so the inspection can be done quickly and employee workload can be planned. Failure to do this may result in employees just 'hanging around' waiting for the inspector to come and inspect the work. There also needs to be special scheduling so that inspectors can access behind the walls. Be careful for work projects where they know the inspector needs to get behind the wall and they plaster over the walls, leaving one spot area left for the inspectors. There can be a lot of defects hidden behind the walls:

- Plumbing shortcuts
- Insects or other wildlife (mice and rats)
- Electrical shortcuts
- Signs of burnt or damaged cabling
- Cracks
- Evidence of damp damage
- Missing insulation
- Mold damage

Various other findings and faults may be hidden behind the walls of your project. Even if the walls are there, an inspector does have the right to make smallish holes to visualize what they need. Additionally, many inspectors now carry endoscopes so they can drill a small hole and run a camera up the wall to ensure code compliance. These holes are easy and quick to patch.

INCIDENCES

Incidences may cause a situation where compensation for injury is agreed to or required. Having correct labor records will ensure that the amount compensated is commensurate with the historical pay of the employee. Of course, the hope is that no incidents occur, but they sometimes do. In order for incidences to be paid by insurance, it is important to have the correct information in place – proper social security number, proper age, dependents, etc. Failure to do so may result in denied claims.

NOTE

1 How to calculate construction labor cost (gobridgit.com).

Chapter 28

Payments and payment auditing

Understanding the payment process is the key to being able to properly understand findings and the amount of money due to the vendors and contractors. As the payment elements are discussed, imagine that you are constructing a layer cake.

Each element belongs to a specific part of the cake and has its own layer or function. Generally, the construction manager accumulates all the costs from all the subcontractors or direct expenses of the project and submits a monthly invoice to the owner. But there are adjustments to be made (Figure 28.1).

A subcontractor will submit a monthly invoice to the contractor. The payment amount and contract type are not necessarily the same arrangement as with the contractor and owner. If a contractor has a lump sum payment with the project owner, they may have cost plus with the subcontractor. Review the contract to be sure.

In exchange for making payment to the subcontractor, the contractor is entitled to full reimbursement plus a fee for administrative and overhead costs. This fee should be considered the icing on the cake. But there needs to be some control to ensure that the contractor is not going to collect payment and then leave without finishing the project.

We take a slice of the cake away and we call this retainage. Retainage is most likely 10% of the payment amount. It is withheld until such time as the contractor has substantially completed all the work (this is usually around 95%, check the contract to be sure). Now if the subcontractor used a contractor that would be a sub-subcontractor and that layer will follow in a similar way.

The contractor has a layer of direct costs (such as material or small expenses) that in turn he submits to the project owner. The contractor gets a fee on top of those expenses and the owner withholds a portion as retainage. This is the top layer of the cake.

Because there are so many fees for overhead and withholdings for retainage, it is important to understand which layer the payment comes from so that the correct adjustments can be made. Here is an example:

DOI: 10.1201/9781003461487-29

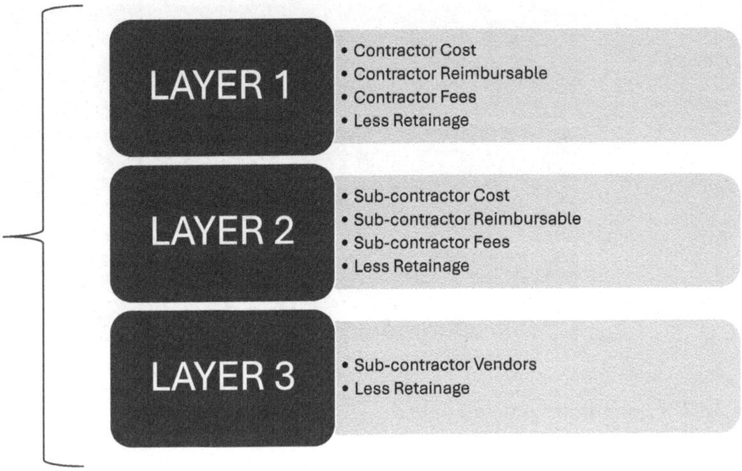

Figure 28.1 Payment structure.

- Contractor A receives a fee of 4.5% for all costs and is subject to a retainage of 10%.
- He contracts with Company B to provide a marble stand in the main lobby.
- B installed the stand, but they cannot engrave the top of the stand, they contract this out to Company C.
- Company B gets 3.5% in fee and is subject to retainage of 10%.

Company C submits a bill for $10,000 for the engraving. They originally bid $20,000 for the whole job; this represents half of the work. Here is how the payment goes up the line.

- Company B pays Company C $9,000 which is $10,000 minus the retainage of 10% ($1000).
- Company B submits an invoice to Company A for $9000 plus $315 for their 3.5% fee.
- Company A pays $8,383.50 to Company B and retains $931.50 for retainage.
- Company A submits an invoice to the project owner of $8,383.50 plus a fee of 4.5% for a total of $8,760.76.
- Owner pays Company A, $7,884.69 which is the $8,760.76 minus the 10% retainage.

The flow looks something like Figure 28.2.

When calculating payments, fee is added first and then retainage is calculated on the new total. Now, assume an audit determines that the correct bid for Company C was only $18,000. That does not mean that there is an

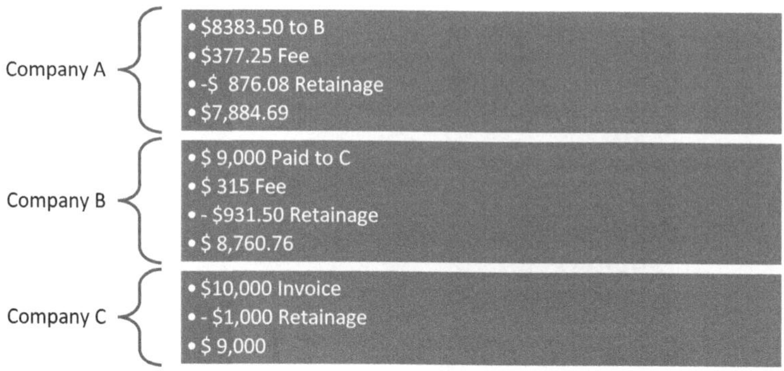

Figure 28.2 Payment structure applied.

overpayment of $2,000 as you need to reverse the process and add the figures back in. Here is what I mean:

- The auditor claims that the correct bid for Company C is $18,000, not $20,000. They billed for half of the work so the overcharge is $2000 * .5 or $1000 but it is not done there.
- Remember Company B got a fee of 3.5% and
- Contractor A got a fee of 4.5%. Therefore,
  - the total overpayment becomes $1000
  - plus B's fees of $35
  - plus A's fee of $46.57 (1,350 * 4.5%).
  - Add those fees back and it becomes a total overpayment of $1081.57.

Normally it is not worth the complications to recalculate the retainage as it will catch up with itself on the next payment, nor is the amount usually material.

In the above example, you get a sense of how payments actually flow. You can also see how costs are intertwined with one another. I recommend that you do as much of your workpapers automated, it will make things easier in the long run. For example, equipment may be charged at a fixed rate. If the equipment was charged at the wrong rate, the auditor may need to go back, find all instances of the equipment and make an adjustment. This can be very timely and result in inaccurate results. If you have an auditor who is good with spreadsheets and linking spreadsheets across one another, this is a great task to ask them to do. It may also be wise to walk through it as a team.

Many construction projects bill using a just-in-time method. Materials are billed as used, not when ordered. If there is concern over supply chain disruptions, there may be an agreement to change this. There should be a way to ensure that materials ordered are used on that project. Especially if expenses are front loaded. (This means that they are charged before use.) Whether this is allowed or not will depend on how the payment clause is worded in the contract.

When reviewing general contractor payments, all monthly contract payments should be selected. It should not be done as a sample. Consistency from bill to bill should be audited as there are many places to hide unauthorized expenses. Additionally, auditing the payments, as a whole, will let you know how the project flows.

When auditing payments you want to use the RADIO criteria. There are five aspects you want to audit:

R – Payment is calculated as per the contractual terms and expenses submitted are REIMBURSABLE per the terms of the contract.
A – Payments are arithmetically correct and ACCURATE back to supporting documentation.
D – Payment components are DOCUMENTED and there is a receipt for expenses incurred.
I – Payments are for expenses that can be proven as being INCURRED. If not, there is an agreement (preferably written) to pay the expense in advance.
O – Payments are submitted in a logical ORDER. This is where data analytics can come in to play.

Here are some examples I have identified in past projects:

1. Invoices were submitted for the payment of bonuses to employees. The contract specifically excluded bonuses, training, and sick pay.
2. Mathematical inaccuracy is common in projects. Many will not bother to even check the math, especially if the invoice looks electronic. However, I have found many errors here. Especially check math when looking at extension prices times a certain number of units. Audit the extension price, as well.
3. Invoices were submitted showing normal business set-up expenses and material for the site trailer. The office did not appear to be set up with new equipment. When asked about receipts for any of the items, the contractor did not have access to any.
4. Invoices were submitted for expenses. Expenses were allowed per the contract. Submissions were raised however, as the receipts were for the year before and not the current year. The project was not active in the year prior. The payments had not been incurred for this project. A review of the prior project showed that these invoices were specifically denied for reimbursement.
5. Painting charges were submitted and 80% of the painting budget was already used, although there were only walls on about 20% of the project. All the walls were exterior walls, no interior walls had existed.

Further investigation showed that some earlier trades were at or close to their maximum. The contractor dumped additional funds into the painting cost center, hoping they would catch up on costs.

Decisions over renting equipment versus buying equipment should also be made and may be more evident of an issue during the audit. One specific rented equipment is steel plates. This is used to bridge gaps in the site that will eventually be replaced by a building, foundations or streets to the site. The rental price is about $35 a week. But when multiplied by the amount needed and the length of time needed, the $35 adds up. Buying these plates will cost around $350–400.

Thirty-five dollars a week for 10 weeks, and you will have paid for the plate. The project itself is generally more than 10 weeks. The plates are usually used for the whole project. Usually, it's cheaper to buy the plates than to rent them long-term. Many have argued that they have no need for them afterward. Solutions can be applied. Plates can be thrown out at the end of the project, resold, sold back to contractors, or saved for future projects. If the decision is made to rent anyway, that is okay, but the auditor should still see proof that the conversation happened and that the agreement was to rent. This is not the only equipment that should be treated this way so a review of small equipment and material should be done.

CASE STUDY

We were working on an audit of a high-profile construction project. It was January and it was snowing. The workers were doing a lot of administrative work, waiting for the snow to stop. The office where the workers were assigned was nearby, but we shared a coffee area.

I was auditing payroll and noticed that the workers received generous end-of-year bonuses this year. I verified back to the contract that the organization reimbursed for bonuses – normally they do not. Sure enough, the contract stated that bonuses would be reimbursed. So, I would need some additional work on my payroll testing to test bonus amounts.

I figured this would be the perfect time to refill my coffee cup. As I was there, two workers were talking about the holidays and grumbling about the dreaded holiday credit card spending. I overheard one state that with this project, they expected the bonuses would be generous. The other worker snickered and said, 'Yeah I think my bonus paid for stuffing one stocking this year - the dog's!' Confused by this, I asked them how much they got and their names. I took that back to the payroll I was testing. The bonus on the payroll report was significantly more than what the workers got.

There is a happy ending. We went back to the vendor with the findings and gave them a choice to refund the money or pay the employees the bonus on the payroll report. The employees got the bonus, and I had fresh coffee every time I went into the coffee room!

Chapter 29

Change orders and auditing change orders

A change order is a written amendment to an existing contract. In essence, each change order is a mini-contract. Work that is added, deleted or changed should be written up in a change order. The change order is broken down into four pieces:

1. The original project information
2. The reason for the change order
3. The impact the change will have on the overall project (cost or time specifically)
4. The responsible party

Yes, just because a change is made, it may not be the responsibility of the owner, though often it gets charged that way. When auditing change orders, it should be audited by someone who is familiar with construction or construction audit. It should not be assigned to an auditor who has not done it before unless they can be supervised and coached. The reason for this advice is that you sometimes need construction experience to understand why the change was issued and what it means. However, if procedures are working correctly, that decision has already been documented.

CAUSES OF CHANGE ORDERS

Change orders can come up for various reasons and the reason should be clearly marked on the change order. The most common reason is site conditions. This means that they found something that required fixing before continuing the project. This could be anything from contaminated soil to building code asking for a change. There are various other reasons – architectural error, unable to get right material, change of plans, etc.

DOI: 10.1201/9781003461487-30

BEST PRACTICES

Procedures should be in place and these procedures should be documented, enforced and included in the contract.

- The first thing that should happen is the change needs to be categorized as emergency or routine. Though the procedures are similar, emergency change orders have a quick-to-approve path. Emergency needs to be defined. An emergency change order would be a change that has to be made quickly so as not to impact people or the overall project. Examples of this are: water main break, structural collapse, scaffolding repair, etc.
- If it is deemed an emergency then the work should be carried out after getting verbal agreement from the architect and program manager. Within 24 hours, the contractor or project manager shall file a change order form. The form may be different than the one I show but it should still have at a minimum, the reason for the change and the impact on the project. For an emergency change order, as part of the description, it should include a note as to who okayed the work.
- For a non-emergency change order, a change order form should be filled out. It should explain why the work is being done and the impact on the project. After that, whether an emergency or non-emergency the process merges.
- The change should be presented to the change control board. The change control board should meet often, even if it is a phone or Zoom meeting. They should meet once a week or more. The project manager should be at the meeting to brief the board on the specifics of the change. If the change was an emergency, it should still be presented but it should mention that it has already been done. The change control board can take one of three actions: approve the change order as stated, deny the change order, or ask for modification.
- Any changes that are approved should be noted on the month-end report. When auditing change orders you may hear the term PCO or potential change orders. This is simply a non-emergency change order that has yet to be approved by the change control board.

CHANGE CONTROL BOARD

Members of the change control board should consist of an executive or a designated person of the executive, facility's management and a clinical person. The project manager should NOT be a voting member of the change control board. A clinical person should be an assigned end user who knows how the end product will be used. There should be a representative from all groups affected by the changes on the agenda, management or non-management alike. It should include one representative from all groups affected by the change. If there is a construction controller, they may sit on the change control board.

Project managers should not be voting members of the change control board. They are not independent of the process. Similarly, external project team members may attend the call but should not be voting members.

Members of the board should know what change orders will be discussed before the call. This gives them the chance to research any claims and come up with a valid reason for the approval or denial. It also gives them a chance to ask questions ahead of the meeting to get the information they need to make an informed decision. They may want to know about the contingency budget. That is acceptable, however, this should be done away from the eyes and ears of external project members.

After the meeting, all change orders and their disposition should be recorded on a change control log. Even those changes that were denied should be on the list. This will help ensure that the members don't try to resubmit change orders. As part of the audit, a copy of the change control log shall be obtained. Negative change orders are money coming back or being credited to the organization. If there are any 'negative' change orders, the auditor should follow the change order through to ensure that the organization gets the credit promised.

CHANGE ORDER ABUSE

Change order abuse is very common in construction. It is even joked about in the industry. A common photo that hangs in many construction projects shows a yacht that says Change order with a tiny dinghy next to it called Original Contract. Unfortunately, no one knows who took the picture so I could not get permission to copy it here. Google it though, it comes up.

Because of the sheer volume of change orders and the haste to get them approved, change orders do not go through thorough scrutiny and it is 'easy' to collude on fraud and abuse of the change order process. This can be done by charging different amounts than normally agreed for material and services. Normally with change orders, costs are actual costs but they can fiddle with labor hours, material needs or other elements to add a few extras. I have even seen change orders for 'expediting services' which was a fancy way to say they bribed officials to get a certificate issued. Of course, if they said Bribe, it may have been questioned.

CASE STUDY 1

While renovating units in a residential facility the contractor had ordered specific stoves. These were asked for by the owner. The stoves were purchased and installed without issue. There were about 900 stoves. In fact, the contractor was proud of the fact that they had purchased the stoves at a discount. But there was a small issue. The stoves had attached exhaust hoods on them but there is a small piece of plastic that covers the vent. These were missing. Audit was told that in order to pass code, you need this piece of plastic. This was never verified.

The plastic piece was about 4 inches by 1 inch. Change orders were issued 10 at a time for $50 per piece of plastic. If you ordered it from the warehouse, the cost would be less than $2.00 each. If you bought it from Amazon the price increases to $3.50. When asked why they split the change orders, the reason given was you could only order 10 at a time so they issued one change order for each order. Audit noted that the first 30 were ordered one week before the rest. This was probably done to 'test' the waters and see how much scrutiny each one got. I routinely 'shop' for specific items when doing a construction audit to get an idea of how much it costs. As a trade, I would expect that the contractor can get the goods much cheaper than the price I could come up to. In fact, each year Home Depot publishes a catalog for contractors. I like to get them and keep them in my audit library for exactly this reason. It helps also when debating the price with the contractor.

Sample Change Order

CHANGE ORDER

Date: Change order number: _____

(Contractor) is directed to make the following changes:

Reason for Change:

Responsible Party

Owner ___________
Architect ___________
Contractor ___________
Other ____________

Cost for Change:

Original Contract Amount	$_______________
Total Prior Changes	$_______________
Total Amount of the Change	$_______________
Total Contract Amount with all changes	$_______________

Potential Delays	_______________
Original Estimated Completion	_______________
New Estimated Completion	_______________

Contractor

____

Change Control Board _______________
Approval Date _______________

The goal of every project should be to keep change orders to a minimum but unfortunately, eliminating them all together is a near impossible task.

CASE STUDY 2

A local hospital was building a new surgical suite. The scope of the project was a reception desk, a patient holding ward, three new operating rooms and a recovery suite. There were designs done by the architect and they were reviewed by members of the project team. When they went to build the operating room, they noticed that the lights were not able to be placed exactly where the plans said. There was existing infrastructure in the way. Contractors decided to move the lights a few inches to the right. The first surgery was scheduled but once the patient was in, there was a problem. By moving the lights, the surgical field was altered. The lights were pointed at the patient's waist instead of their chest. The contractor was new to hospital construction and did not realize that this change would have an impact like that. Additionally, there was no clinical person on the change control.

Chapter 30

Special considerations

With each audit, the program needs to be customized and may require that the auditor spend a lot of time thinking outside the box. Even if a member of the project team, a lot of the challenge comes from having to fix problems.

NDAS

Non-disclosure agreements (NDAs) are very important in construction. Think of how many times you may have been in an office and a vendor comes into the room. There are times when we continue conversations and ignore them as if they were not there. Many times, a contractor can be working on a ceiling or nearby and may walk through a used office. They may even be part of the punch list team. The amount of information they can garner can be substantial and dangerous if leaked.

UPSKILLING OF AUDITORS

Construction audit is not necessarily a popular type of audit but many organizations are doing it now. The National Association of Construction Auditors was formed to help upskill auditors and to develop the importance of construction audit. Through training programs and networking, NACA helps facilitate how auditors in other fields can enter the field of construction audit. It is a long-running commitment to audit and allows a lot of opportunity to have exposure to executive management. It can also allow them to see project management at work. For those who are interested, they may even apply to become a Project Management Professional (PMP). Many of the skills needed for PMP can come from the work that audit does in project management and capital improvement audits.

DOI: 10.1201/9781003461487-31

PROFESSIONAL SKEPTICISM

Professional skepticism is a term used to describe a critical assessment of audit evidence. It is an attitude that includes a questioning mind and being alert for errors, frauds and/or misstatements. As construction or project auditors, that is exactly what we do. We can look at the documentation and trust what we see, but we need to verify as well.

SOLICITING HELP FROM OTHERS

Just like we use outsiders on our projects, it is okay to use outsiders on our project audits. Outside resources may be needed: architects, estimators and construction attorneys. It is perfectly acceptable to solicit help from outsiders just ensure that any Audit Reports state that certain work was done by outsiders and include:

- Scope of services provided
- How Audit verified their expertise
- What did it cost to use the service
- Why did Audit feel that the use of the services was needed

MANAGEMENT ACTION PLANS

Management Action Plans may need to be solicited. In accepting action plans, Audit should not be looking to add any red tape, unless absolutely necessary. There is enough paperwork already! In fact, if Audit can remove any red tape it will enhance the collaborative relationship between Audit and Project Management.

REMEMBER THE GOAL

The goal of a construction audit is not to play 'Gotcha!'. It is about ensuring:

- Financial accuracy and transparency
- Looking at efficiency and effectiveness
- Providing quality information to the right parties at the right time
- Compliance with contracts
- Identifying and addressing the risks
- Regulatory compliance
- Stakeholder piece of mind
- Learning process

Remember the lessons learned phase. There are many things that the organization may be doing right, there may be things that they are struggling with, and there are things that could be done better. Self-reflection is the key to help ensure a quality audit and to improve processes going further. What we learn from the construction may be affecting other areas or can help other areas. It is okay to provide lessons learned across the organization and not just for the project under audit.

RECOVERING OVERPAYMENTS

Chances are you will find overpayments on the project. Tracking those overpayments is important to prove that the audit is worth the efforts of audit. I have found that when presenting overpayments, contractors will fight it as far as understanding the cause of the issue but they generally will reimburse for overpayments easily and quickly.

Chapter 31

Special types of construction

Is your project 'cutting edge'? Are you trying to:

- Do something that hasn't been done before?
- Use unproven technology?
- Construct a building that requires highly technical or specialist equipment?
- Build in a remote, environmentally hazardous, or harsh environment?
- Do something unusually large or complex?

If your project is 'Cutting Edge' you could be stepping into the unknown. This is not a reason not to go ahead, but such projects often become 'bleeding edge' and hemorrhage resources, money, and time. It could be that the project will provide significant benefits to the organization or even the advancement of mankind (projects for space travel are an example of such projects, pushing the boundaries of science).

What projects might be cutting edge? The following types of projects are among the most difficult I have encountered:

- Power stations (Complex equipment, specifications – especially nuclear)
- Transportation projects (unforeseen environmental factors)
- Medical facilities (after the shell has been built and building is being furnished with equipment, electrical fittings, oxygen lines, etc. especially intensive care, surgical units, and specialist suites such as radiology)
- Unusually tall buildings or unique superstructures

The larger and more complex the project, the more likely unforeseen events will occur, challenges will surface and events that are unknown at the start of the project could occur.

At the time of writing, the UK Government has dramatically changed the scope of a project to develop a new rail link between London and the North of England (stopping at Birmingham rather than the original planned

DOI: 10.1201/9781003461487-32

terminus of Liverpool). The decision to reduce the scope of the project as a result of burgeoning costs attracted much negative comment. (Reputational Risk?) Could this have been prevented? Given that the United Kingdom, like other countries, has faced economic shocks from Covid, the War in the Ukraine, and inflation as well as an inherently complex project it is an illustration of the need for realistic planning and recognition of uncertainty. In this instance, the pockets of the UK Government weren't deep enough to see the project through.

Prudent steps for cutting-edge projects:

If you think your project is cutting edge, then it is especially important to audit the planning process. In particular:

- Board-level oversight.
- Ensure significant contingency funding exists.
    - Treasury management should be closely involved and regularly updated (e.g. supplied with Earned Value Management).
    - Contingency budget is a function of how well you manage projects. Because of its 'experimental' nature, contingency will generally be higher than normal projects.
    - Financial risks should be hedged (e.g. exchange rate hedging if equipment or resources are sourced from overseas).
- Investment appraisals should be verified and particular attention should be given to assumptions.
- Obtain second opinions on areas of high risk – use independent professionals when necessary (estimators to price materials rather than architects).
- Continuous audit of:
    - Accuracy and completeness of stakeholder communication. Especially, risk.
    - Time control.
    - Cost control.
    - Accuracy of project reporting.

If specialist equipment is needed to make a building operational (e.g. backup generator for a data center) the following should be considered:

- Capacity – will the equipment meet current and future needs?
    - Has capacity been agreed with the department responsible for long-term strategic planning?
- Lead time – what is the delivery cycle for medical equipment or generators? This may exceed six months. If you have a place to store it, order it as soon as possible.
- Future replacement – will building allow for potential upgrades and likely developments? For example, if you have a building that will

require special rooms or reinforced flooring to hold equipment, it should be made known at the beginning. This is a consideration we often encounter in hospital construction, especially with radiographic services. This is not as easy as it seems, as sometimes you are constructing for future equipment that does not even exist yet.

Chapter 32

Procuring equipment from abroad

If you will be ordering a lot of material and equipment from overseas, mostly specialty products, there should be a contract in place with the supplier of that equipment. A lot of equipment for power plants comes from China. In the contract, it is possible that you can pre-select a conversion rate or use a form of cryptocurrency. If a pre-selected conversion rate is used, audit should test whether that rate was applied. Additionally, you will want to state that the invoices are in the language of your choice. Good communication is essential with treasury management so that if necessary they can hedge for currency fluctuations.

CASE STUDY 1

While auditing a nuclear facility, they needed to order parts from overseas. The contracts stated that all invoices should be in English and a rate of 10.2 should be used as a currency conversion rate.

I audited the first invoice and realized it was not in English. I had no idea what it was for but realized there was no way to test this. I asked the project team if they had someone who could translate the invoices. They did not. I asked how they performed due diligence on the invoices. They stated they did not check them, since the invoices were not in English and they just accepted them as is. Fortunately, I had a friend who did speak Chinese. She was a fellow auditor but not assigned to this project. I got permission from the client to show the invoices to her.

My friend translated about 30 invoices for me and I brought them back to the office. We checked the 30 we had and there was nothing unusual about the items ordered. Because we did not get all invoices translated we had to assume it was all ok. When I went to cross them off our list of invoices I found that all 30 did not match any amounts on my cash disbursements report. Further investigation revealed that they did not use 10.2 as a currency conversion rate, they used 11.6.

DOI: 10.1201/9781003461487-33

Using Data Analytics we ran all the invoices for that company and this project and did a currency conversion. It took us about an hour to run the reports. The difference was in the millions!

CASE STUDY 2

A company was building new headquarters in Mexico. The company and contractor were located in the USA. This was part of a bigger project to build new offices for the company. It was determined that explosives were needed to do demolition on the site. Due to immigration rules, the contractor was not able to use explosives that they had bought for the US sites. The company decided to purchase the needed dynamite from another Mexican office that they had. The Mexican office ordered and received it. They handed it over to the contractor and the contractor started on the site. The bills came in and on the first invoice, the contractor charged for the demolition used. In fact, the US company had submitted a change order showing that the contractor owed for the explosives as a credit to the first invoice. The first invoice was not pencil copied, as sometimes the first invoice does not get scrutinized as it mostly set up costs. The project auditor, however, knowing about the credit, told accounts payable to keep their eyes open and that if they had any issues, they should run it by him. The auditor went back to the project manager and a correction was quickly made.

Chapter 33

Construction fraud and considerations

The Association of Certified Fraud Examiners defines fraud as 'any activity that relies on deception in order to achieve a gain.'[1] Often fraud is committed because of life issues such as debt, compulsive gambling or other addictions. I have seen many frauds and errors throughout my many years of doing construction. Most have been classified as errors as that is as far as the client wanted to take it. They were more interested in recovering money than prosecuting. There could be various reasons for this: publicity, cost to prosecute, time, etc.

The most effective method of prevention is performing effective pre-employment screening (reference checking for individuals and due diligence for companies). Helping employees with welfare issues via employee assistance programs may also assist in helping some individuals from following a criminal path. The other way to prevent fraud is education: education of the investigator or auditor and education of the back office. To catch a thief, you must think like a thief. As you read the following, put yourself in the fraudster's shoes. Some facts have been changed to protect the privacy of those involved.

LIVING BEYOND MEANS

One of the areas prone for fraud is procurement. It can be done by procurement officials, project managers, facility managers and anyone working on the project. The most common fraud via procurement is kickbacks.

A significant red flag for fraud, and potential for procurement fraud, is an individual who is clearly living beyond their means. If an employee suddenly turns up to work driving a luxury car, buys a new house and takes luxury holidays, it can be an indication of fraud. This could have an innocent explanation such as a lottery win or an inheritance from a wealthy relative.

Many people who commit fraud do not 'think through' how they will spend stolen money. They start to spend their newfound wealth and do not hide it. In many instances they feel compelled to spend it – thinking that

DOI: 10.1201/9781003461487-34

leaving cash lying around will prove fraud. If a fraud is suspected, a change in lifestyle or unexplained wealth may be a further red flag.

Law enforcement investigating fraud has the powers and ability to investigate sources of wealth. Internal fraud investigators within your organization or private investigative services may have the ability to perform a similar investigation: identifying all legitimate sources of income and estimating expenditure. If the individual is living beyond their means, it is not proof of a fraud, but indicative, and can demonstrate motive. In construction audit, I also find that looking at the residence of the home can sometimes be indicative of 'non-cash' kickbacks. This is hard to do as they need to give you access to the home, but sometimes social media will give all the proof you need.

One investigation was done of a well-liked supervisor. There was evidence that she was violating policy about real estate repairs. She was using goods used to repair her real estate portfolio to build a high-end house. The goal was to fix up the house and flip it. The house she purchased belonged to the organization, and they were selling it at auction.

To avoid competition, when marketing the auction, she left this property off the marketing material. Bidders used this material to tour properties ahead of the auction. The day of the auction she was able to bid on the property and there was little competition as the other bidders did not tour this property. When reports from the auction were given back to the organization, they noticed that the house went for a very low amount. They noticed the buyer's name as the mother of the supervisor. Audit was called to investigate.

Audit did initial interviews and realized the supervisor was well-liked. She was always in, always spoiling her staff with cake, donuts, bagels and the works. She even gave generous gifts on their birthday or if they got married. A walkthrough of the property revealed high-end furnishings – a Viking stove, bamboo flooring, pricey granite and fancy woodwork. Auditors recognized the granite as the same granite that was routinely used by the organization. When questioned about this, the supervisor stated she copied it because she fell in love with it through the work she did.

Auditors were able to trace back invoices for some of the furnishings and the granite. All were charged to various projects that the supervisor had worked on. She was terminated and forced to make restitution. The department left behind was left untrusting of one another and eventually had to be reallocated to new departments.

LAYERING FRAUD

When submitting expenses for reimbursement they should normally be submitted by the most senior person. The same holds true for construction. If a group of six people goes to lunch and the organization is there, the organization should pick up the tab and submit for reimbursement. What happens is if a subcontractor or subcontractor of a subcontractor is there, they will pick up the tab. This may seem like just a deviation from policy but there is more to it than that. If the lowest party submits then here's what happens. They submit the expenses for the six people through their invoice. They get paid their G&A fee on top of that. The next party does the same and gets another G&A fee. This continues all the way up to the organization and all those extra G&A fees accumulate.

At the start of this chapter, I explained that the difference between fraud and error was the deceit. This is one of those middle zones where it could be an error, or it could be fraud. Usually this goes down as an 'honest error.'

THE DEDICATED DESIGNER

We worked on a project for medical facilities. There was a building hosting suites of physicians of various specialties. There was also an on-site blood lab and x-rays. There was concern that this project was costing a lot more than other similar projects.

While auditing expenses for the architect, concerns came out that the architect fees were not tapering off and far exceeded what was expected to be paid. Audit was asked to investigate. We asked around as to why this particular architect was used and it turns out he was pre-assigned. Meaning the landlord said we had to use him, and the landlord was reimbursing a percentage of build-out costs. This is a common practice called Leasehold Improvements.

We were looking at bills for the architect and there were a lot of them. He was supposed to only bill once a month. He was billed more like weekly at the beginning and two to three times a week toward the end. This was done so that each invoice was less and it would be an amount that would raise fewer eyebrows.

There was a project manager on the property so we wondered why there were so much costs accumulating after the design was done. We asked him for an electronic copy of the time sheets and were told we would get them shortly. We never received them, so we asked again. We were told he forgot but he would send them right away. Again, we never received them. This went back and forth for several months. Finally, he claimed he did not know how to send them electronically. We agreed for manual time sheets.

While we waited, we pulled some background on the architect and found three main problems:

1. He was not licensed to do architectural work in the state.
2. He had never done commercial work.
3. His taxable income was $750,000 a year yet the client we were working on had already paid out 1.5 million for the year. He was there for two years.

He finally sent a PDF of all the time sheets, knowing that we could not audit them like that. Luckily, one of the auditors was proficient in the Adobe suites and was able to get it converted to Excel. What we found was evidence of fraud.

Once we were able to get the timesheets, we were able to run data analytics on the file. We found there were many instances of duplicate billings, in fact when we totaled the costs of the architect, he worked on average 36 hours a day! While we were preparing to address the issues of the multiple invoices per month and the work hours, he was harassing accounts payable to pay outstanding invoices. He was in essence by passing facilities about the outstanding invoices.

A meeting was held with facilities, the architect, and the Legal team and the architect admitted to fraud and returned $1.8 million to the organization.

CONTAMINATED SOIL

I was called in to do a special request audit due to a complaint that came into the ethics line. The caller lived at an apartment complex and was very irate. Renovations were being done on the complex and she accused workers of polluting the site. We explained that construction does create pollution, but we are trying to keep it to a minimum. She was still not happy and asked why we were pouring the oil from the heavy equipment all over the ground. Confused, we decided to investigate.

I looked at some of the expenses coming in and noticed an uptake in diesel. This is not unusual in and of itself, as it is common that as construction progresses, so does equipment usage. The next day I got to the office early but no one was around to let me in. The office was still looked. I decided to take my breakfast into the courtyard. While there I was people-watching. I saw one of the construction workers arrive. He checked around near the bulldozer. I noticed that he put a tray under the bulldozer and opened up the fuel tank. There he emptied the full tank onto the tray. At first I thought he was siphoning gas, but then I saw why the caller was upset. He poured the oil all over the ground as if he was watering the plants.

I went into the office and decided to go through construction meetings and foreman's reports to see if I could explain this behavior. Then I found it. A week earlier they put in a change order stating they found contaminated soil. When contaminated soil is found, you need to excavate it, send it off for special handling to clean it, and replace the soil with clean backfill. This is a costly process and holds up the progress significantly. The change order was sent back asking for soil samples to go to the lab.

To make the soil look contaminated, they contaminated it themselves. The worker had a brother who specialized in cleaning soil. Sure enough, that is where they were sending the soil to be cleaned. This case also emphasized the importance of advertising the fraud hotline, even for sites not near your office.

NOTE

1 Fraud 101 – What is Fraud? https://www.acfe.com/fraud-resources/fraud-101-what-is-fraud 101 – November 26, 2023.

Chapter 34

Closing thoughts

Construction projects are a long-term commitment of the organization. Construction audits are also a long-term commitment. Throughout this book I left you with a lot to ponder. But as a construction team improves through learning curve, the same will happen with construction audits. Here are some top ten takeaways to help you build that foundation and ensure a quality project.

1. Each project is unique, each risk matrix is unique and each audit is unique.
2. Build a strong contract to help protect the organization. As an auditor, make sure you read and understand the contract, even if it means carving out a large chunk of time to do so.
3. Safety is important on site. Sites are full of risk to personal safety but with a minimum amount of effort and increased focus, it is possible to ensure workers go home each night, safely.
4. Communication is the key to a successful project, and part of that communication is audit to the project team. Be compassionate but firm! There are a lot of moving parts, make sure you focus on the overall picture.
5. Identify the risks and think about mitigating controls, even if it requires some creative and out-of-the-box solutions.
6. Remember the criteria for project success:
   - Cost
   - Time
   - Quality
   - Function
   - Scope
   - Safety

   And remember the priority will change; check the project charter.
7. It is okay to ask for help.
8. Know your vendors and know your project team, including how they were selected.

DOI: 10.1201/9781003461487-35

9. Start from the beginning. Depending on the scope of the project or to understand the scope of the audit, go all the way back to the investment decision phase.
10. You can do it! Reach out if you need help or with any questions, you can find this author at denise.cicchella@auspiciumco.com. You can reach the National Association of Construction Auditors at 1-888-702-1059.

Thank you for taking the time to read this and together we can help make construction projects that are more effective and economical and that provide greater levels of success.

Index

Pages in *italics* refer to figures and pages in **bold** refer to tables.